Developing and Presenting a Professional Portfolio in Early Childhood Education

Second Edition

Nancy W. Wiltz

Towson University

Ocie Watson-Thompson

Towson University

Hannah S. Cawley

Towson University

Heather Skelley

Towson University

Boston, Massachusetts
Columbus, Ohio

Between the time website information is gathered and then published, it is not unusual for some sites to have closed. Also, the transcription of URLs can result in typographical errors. The publisher would appreciate notification where these errors occur so that they may be corrected in subsequent editions.

This book was printed and bound by Bind Rite Graphics. The cover was printed by Phoenix Color Corp.

10 9 8 7 6 5 4 3 2 1
ISBN-13: 978-0-13-714914-8
ISBN-10:   0-13-714914-X

PREFACE

This manual has been developed to assist preservice teachers in early childhood education develop a professional portfolio. The book uses a step-by-step approach and numerous examples to assist early childhood majors in successfully developing a paper and/or an electronic professional teaching portfolio. Each chapter is designed to support the development of the professional portfolio in the same way we support our Towson University Interns through this process.

Chapter 1 explains the use of professional portfolio, defines what portfolio is, establishes a rationale for completing a portfolio, and explains the phases of the portfolio process. Chapter 2 explicates the principles and standards used by early childhood educators to structure a portfolio that illustrates competencies of beginning teachers in our field. Chapter 3 guides you in setting up your portfolio. Chapter 4 explains what artifacts are and how they are used to describe what you know and what you can do. Chapter 5 addresses electronic portfolios. Chapter 6 directs you in developing a strong philosophy statement. Chapter 7 addresses the important task of writing effective reflective narratives, and differentiates between a caption and a reflective narrative. Chapters 8, 9, and 10 go through the developmental process. These chapters explain collecting, selecting, evaluating, and presenting your portfolio. The final chapter addresses what comes next. You are now no longer a student, but a teacher. How did the portfolio process help you become the teacher you are now?

Acknowledgments

The authors wish to acknowledge the support of the students and faculty in the Department of Early Childhood Education and the College of Education at Towson University. Portions of this book were made possible, in part, from Summer Research Fellowships from the Faculty Development and Research Committee at Towson University. All the artifacts included come from our students, who have generously allowed us to use their work. In particular we would like to thank: Mrs. Michelle Clemovich, Mrs. Gerry DePetris, Elizabeth Eagling, Lindsey Franck, Jenna Grace, Megan Higdon, Dr. Judith Guerrero, Dr. Mubina Kirmani, Courtney Lamb, Jenn Maikin, Melissa Martin, Natalie Morris, Kathleen Landis-Mullins, Dr. Karen Murphy, Barbara Pohlman, Nicole Pulchino, Jennifer Rick, Miguel Rodriguez, James Rock, Sarah Rybka, Katie Runyon, Mrs. Barbara Steele, Jenn Warner, and Alexandra Welsh.

We would like to thank the reviewers: Regina M. Adesanya, New Jersey City University; Elizabeth M. Elliott, Florida Gulf Coast University; Linda Fitzharris, College of Charleston; Carmelita Lomeo-Smrtic, Mohawk Valley Community College; and Mary Thompson Price, University of Houston. Finally we would like to thank our editor, Julie Peters, at Pearson/Merrill/Prentice Hall, whose assistance was invaluable.

ABOUT THE AUTHORS

Nancy W. Wiltz, Ph. D.

Nancy W. Wiltz earned a B.S. in Education at the University of Missouri-Columbia and taught fifth grade for five years before staying home with young children. Returning to graduate school in 1991, she earned an M.A. and a Ph. D. in Curriculum and Instruction at the University of Maryland, College Park. In 1999, she joined the Early Childhood Education faculty at Towson University, and is now an Associate Professor there. She teaches Pre Primary and Primary curriculum courses to students in their final professional semesters. In these courses, she enjoys helping students develop their final showcase and interview portfolios, and evaluates portfolios during students' final three semesters in the Early Childhood Education Program.

Ocie Watson-Thompson, Ed. D.

Dr. Ocie Watson-Thompson, a native of Alabama, was first an elementary school teacher, and has taught for 15 of her 25 years in teacher education at Towson University. Her specialty is Curriculum and Instruction with concentrations in special education, literacy, and diversity. As the "guru" of portfolios at Towson University, she teaches the portfolio course, as well as courses ranging from Introduction to Early Childhood Education to the final capstone Student Teaching Seminar. This range helps her clearly articulate the progressive work that goes into portfolio development and presentation. Dr. Watson-Thompson is an Associate Professor at Towson University where she currently chairs the Department of Early Childhood Education.

Heather Skelley, M. S.

Heather Skelley received her Bachelor's and Master's degrees from Towson University, and is currently a full-time Lecturer in the Department of Early Childhood Education, where she teaches reading, literacy, and curriculum courses. She is a former Pre-Kindergarten, first-, and second-grade classroom teacher in the Baltimore County Public Schools. She spent two years as a Professional Developer with the *Fund for Educational Excellence*, and currently is a professional developer for *Children's Literacy Infinitive*, a nonprofit organization that provides literacy staff development for teachers in urban school districts. Not only has she modified and written curriculum in reading for the State of Maryland, but also she and Hannah Cawley have co-authored several online courses.

Hannah Smith Cawley, M. S.

Hannah Smith Cawley joined the Department of Early Childhood Education faculty at Towson University as a full time Lecturer in 2003. She teaches a variety of courses in Early Childhood Education, ranging from the introductory course to the Student Teaching Seminar. Mrs. Cawley hails from Maine and completed her Master's degree at the University of Illinois, Champaign-Urbana. This range of experiences allows her to bring a fresh and critical eye to the portfolio development process. With Heather Skelley, she has developed several online courses including *Human Growth and Development* and *Introduction to Early Childhood Education*. She is also a university liaison to a cluster of Professional Development Schools in Baltimore County.

TABLE OF CONTENTS

CHAPTER 1: An Introduction to Your Portfolio   1

CHAPTER 2: Using Teaching Standards to Organize Your Portfolio   7

CHAPTER 3: Setting Up Your Portfolio   17

CHAPTER 4: Identifying Artifacts   31

CHAPTER 5: Electronic Portfolios   39

CHAPTER 6: Developing a Philosophy of Education Statement   45

CHAPTER 7: Writing Your Reflective Narrative   57

CHAPTER 8: The Collection Phase   75

CHAPTER 9: The Selection Phase: Choosing Artifacts for the Showcase Portfolio   85

CHAPTER 10: The Final Phase: Preparing, Assessing, and Presenting Your Portfolio   89

CHAPTER 11: Taking Your Portfolio to the Next Step   105

CHAPTER 1

AN INTRODUCTION TO YOUR PORTFOLIO

The use of a professional teaching portfolio comes from the field of art, writing, and architecture, where professionals in those fields collect and display samples of work to showcase their talents and skills (Glatthorn, 1996). The idea of using portfolios to document proficiency in teaching is embedded in those traditions, and has become increasingly valued and used in teacher education in recent years (Costantino, De Lorenzo, & Kobrinski, 2006). Portfolio development is considered a worthwhile process for documenting teaching performance, fostering professional growth, and facilitating reflective thinking. Portfolios—either paper or electronic—are one approach in determining the effectiveness of aspiring teachers. When used with other forms of assessment, portfolios provide a broad and complete picture of the pre-service teacher. Since most states have moved to standards-based programs, built on "the idea that educators need to present evidence of their competence relative to standards" (Ashford & Deering, 2003, p. 22), portfolios have became the "customary method for displaying teaching competence and content-area knowledge" (Rieman & Okrasinski, 2007, p. 2).

What is a Portfolio?

Preparing you, the student, to be thoughtful and reflective is an important aspect of both teaching and learning. Your construction of teacher knowledge is emphasized through experiences that include planning, teaching, assessing, discussing, and reflecting on understanding in a variety of ways. In line with Dewey's notion of reflective inquiry (1933/1998), you are encouraged to acquire and apply knowledge simultaneously. In short, you learn by doing. "Since much of what a teacher knows and . . . does in a classroom is not easily measured with traditional paper/pencil assessments, [portfolio is], with ever-increasing frequency, surfacing as a popular tool for documenting teacher preparation, in-service performance, and professional development" (Martin, 1999, p. 4).

A portfolio is "an envelope of the mind" (Dietz, 1995)—an organized collection of artifacts, evidences, and reflections that represent progressive progress toward professional growth, continuous learning, and "achieved competence in the complex act called teaching" (Campbell, Cignetti, Melenyzer, Nettles, & Wyman, 2007, p. 4). Portfolios are "ongoing assessments that are composed of purposeful collections that examine achievement, effort, improvement, and processes, such as selecting, comparing, sharing, self-evaluation, and goal setting (Tierney, Carter, & Desai as cited in Johnson & Rose, 1997, p. 6).

In education, portfolios document the totality of the college experience. As you change throughout your college years, portfolios help you carefully look at your teaching performance, encourage your professional growth, and contribute to reflective thinking. A portfolio is more than a scrapbook, and not merely a container for storing and displaying evidence of a teacher's knowledge and skills. A teaching portfolio is tangible evidence of knowledge, skills, attitudes, and dispositions. As a structured, selective collection of work that illustrates an individual's talents as a teacher/learner (Doolittle, 1994), portfolios also assess skills, understandings, and processes, and use a variety of evidence to record growth over time (Klenowski, 2002).

There is not a set formula for preparing one's portfolio, and no two look alike. By selecting evidence of your individual strengths, a unique picture of you comes to life. However, all portfolios create a context for your teaching experiences. They provide formative evaluation in the form of self-improvement and achievement, and include rationales for the chosen artifacts. Portfolios allow you to assess strengths, reflect on goals, and identify areas for further growth. Summative evaluation occurs at the end of a two- or four-year process when you communicate a personal portrait of yourself and chronicle your development to a team of professors and teachers. Your presentation is tailored to using a variety of methods and multiple sources to document those specific standards that have been satisfactorily met.

Not only does the portfolio serve as an instrument of your growth and development as a pre-service intern and an emerging teacher, it also provides important information for the assessment of an Early Childhood Education Program. It serves to depict the knowledge, skills, attitudes, dispositions, and ultimately, the presentation, needed for effective teachers of young children. As an authentic form of assessment, portfolios are experiential, helping you as a student to achieve mastery in discovery and problem solving. Portfolios differ from other types of assessment in the following ways:

> (1) Portfolios allow the student to select from multiple sources of evidence gathered in authentic settings.
> (2) Portfolio development requires decision making on the part of the developer.
> (3)   Portfolio assists in determining future professional goals.
> (http://www.sitesupport.org/module1/teacherreflection.htm/).

What is the Purpose of Portfolio?

The main purpose of the portfolio is to document your growth and development as an emerging teacher. It is a way that you can see yourself grow, develop, and change over time. Production of a portfolio always involves both process and a product. The process includes the systematic collection, selection, and reflection of evidence that documents the continuous growth in competencies identified by internal and external professional standards. As a product, a portfolio is a purposeful collection of evidence selected to provide documentation of professional growth and achievement that is arranged in an easily manageable format. Choosing and organizing text, images, photographs, sounds, video, and other artifacts to represent one's teaching beliefs and experiences involves a reflective process "that provides the greatest opportunities for professional understanding and self-assessment" (http://www.sitesupport.org/module1/teacherreflection.htm, p.1).

While the portfolio's primary purpose is to document and support the attainment of identified competencies, there are additional values. The production of a portfolio allows for many levels of personal and professional growth:

> • Initiates a mindset of learning as a lifelong endeavor
> • Develops and supports reflective thinking
> • Engenders collaboration between all professional partners (interns, mentor teachers, University faculty)
> • Places responsibility on you to shape your own professional destiny
> • Presents a more authentic picture of acquired knowledge, skills, attitudes, and dispositions
> • Provides multiple data sources to document growth and achievement.
> • Facilitates goal setting

- Integrates theory and practice
- Contributes to and fosters best practice

Stages or Phases of the Portfolio Process

Colleges of Education, students, and school systems have developed many types of portfolios. The five types described in this book are commonly found throughout the literature, although terminology may differ. While some books refer to these as "types" of portfolios, we emphasize that they are really stages or phases of developing because each portfolio type emphasizes growth and change over time. Obviously, what you include in your portfolio depends upon the purpose of your portfolio, the level of development and professionalism, and the audience for whom it is created.

Collection Portfolio—A Collection Portfolio is merely a compilation of evidence that can include any and all college-level experiences and activities related to your growth. Ideally, this type of portfolio is begun in your first early childhood courses, where the emphasis is on collecting a variety of artifacts that document skills, knowledge, dispositions, and experiences that support your desire or potential to be a successful early childhood educator. Artifacts in this stage might include observations, interviews, article reflection papers, research papers, PowerPoint presentations, journals, projects, and assignments that feature work from early childhood theorists.

Developmental Portfolio—The Developmental Portfolio is a continuing collection of evidence that reflects developing competencies over a longer period of time. While you are still collecting artifacts, you are now past the early coursework and are focusing more on classroom teaching, acquiring management skills, involving learners in active inquiry, and increasing your interactions with other professionals in early childhood education. Instead of just turning in a research paper or a mock lesson plan, you now ask yourself, "How does this impact what I do with children?" This type of portfolio is sometimes called a working portfolio (Martin, 1999; Costantino et al., 2006) or a process portfolio (Antonek, McCormick, & Donato, 1997) because it reflects work in progress. A working portfolio is "a collection of teaching evidence and reflections displayed as paper or digital assets that provide ongoing documentation of a teacher candidate's growth at various benchmarks throughout the teacher education program" (Costantino et al., 2006, p. 169). But the developmental portfolio is not yet a polished document.

Artifacts here, in addition to those mentioned for the Collection Portfolio, might include classroom observations, child development studies, pieces of reflective writing, a variety of lesson plans, samples or lists of instructional materials created for teaching, thematic units, and projects involving parents and/or the community.

Assessment Portfolio—The Assessment Portfolio is commonly used in academic settings, especially teacher credentialing institutions, as well as for national teacher certification (Jones & Shelton, 2006). This portfolio type is designed to show competence in all areas of the specified criteria, which is often a set of professional standards adopted by your school, district, or state. Ultimately you are assessed on how well you meet the standards that measure student learning outcomes, and your readiness for the teaching profession.

An assessment portfolio pays much less attention to collection, and more attention to selection and reflection of evidence from a variety of sources. At this point, you review the existing artifacts in the portfolio you have created. You may want to strengthen your portfolio by paying in-depth attention to required criteria, clarifying links between your narrative reflection and the chosen artifact, and refining artifacts to better meet the indicators of each standard. Self-assessment and feedback from faculty, mentor teachers, and peers may help you with this process.

Showcase Portfolio—The Showcase Portfolio is a "polished collection of exemplary documents and reflective entries that highlight an in-service teacher's best work and accomplishments" (Costantino et al., 2006, p.169). This type of portfolio demands much more intensity on selection and reflection of evidence relative to identified standards and criteria. Take time to sort through your artifacts. Choose a balanced selection of artifacts that document learning in all curricular areas and under all professional standards. Present a consistent, cumulative, and comprehensive profile of yourself that confirms your competencies and effectiveness, and that showcases your very best work. This type of portfolio is often used in discussions with professors, peers, and mentor teachers to identify areas of strengths and continued growth.

Interview Portfolio—The Interview Portfolio is usually a subset of your best work from the collection, developmental, assessment, and showcase portfolios. Sometimes this is called a product portfolio (Antonek et al., 1997) because the process has now resulted in an end product that identifies and supports effective, professional competencies, provides evidence specific to a particular district and/or position desired, and communicates evidence of your readiness to enter the teaching profession. Sometimes an interview portfolio is known as a presentation portfolio because it is compiled "for the expressed purpose of giving others an effective and easy-to-read portrait of your professional competence" (Campbell et al., 2007, p. 4). An interview portfolio is selective and streamlined so that your material can be viewed in a timely manner. Reduce your number of artifacts to only those that support and document your strength and accomplishments as a teacher.

Activity 1-1

Now that you have an understanding of what a portfolio is, its purpose, why you would use it, and the various stages you will go through to develop a portfolio, answer the following questions:
- What is a portfolio?
- Why would you develop a professional portfolio?
- What is the value of portfolio development?
- How do your envision your portfolio evolving through the stages?
- What unique characteristics or skills do you have that you want to be showcased?

Summary

This chapter has introduced you to the portfolio concept as a means of assisting you in developing a professional portfolio. You have learned that portfolios in teacher education are often based upon one or more sets of standards that you will be asked to meet. Portfolios also become an authentic assessment process whereby you ultimately demonstrate your individuality, creativity, professionalism, organizational skills, writing ability, computer skills, leadership, and potential to succeed as a teacher. Through the descriptions of the various stages in the portfolio process, you have learned that portfolios are not distinct types, but rather are overlapping in stages and phases in a developmental process.

Suggested Web Sites

Johns Hopkins University and Morgan State University provide a step-by-step description of the portfolio process, additional readings, activities to support portfolio development, and examples/models of electronic portfolio. http://www.sitesupport.org/.htm.

TeacherVision includes information on learning how to design and implement a portfolio, as well as concrete ideas on what to include in a professional portfolio for teachers. http://www.teachervision.fen.com/teacher-training/curriculum-planning/20153.html

This site offers an abundance of information with step-by-step instructions in developing an educator's professional portfolio. http://www.uleth.ca/edu/undergrad/fe/pdf/portfolioguide.pdf

Washington State University provides this site that includes a general format, outline of a teaching portfolio, examples of teaching portfolios, and references. http://www.wsu.edu/provost/teaching.htm

References

Antonek, J. L., McCormick, D. E., & Donato, R. (1997). The student-teacher portfolio as autobiography: Developing a professional identity. *The Modern Language Journal, 81* (1), 15-27.

Ashford, A., & Deering, P. (2003). *Middle level teacher preparation: The impact of the portfolio experience on teachers' professional development.* Paper presented at the Annual meeting of the American Educational Research Association, Chicago, IL.

Campbell, D. M., Cignetti, P. B., Melenyzer, B. J., Nettles, D. H., & Wyman, R. M. (2007). *How to develop a professional portfolio: A manual for teachers* (4th ed.). Boston: Allyn & Bacon.

Costantino, P. M., DeLorenzo, M. N., & Kobrinski, E. J. (2006). *Developing a professional teaching portfolio: A guide for success* (2nd ed.). Boston: Allyn & Bacon.

Dewey, J. (1933/1998). *How we think: A restatement of the relation of reflective thinking to the educative process.* Boston: Houghton Mifflin Company.

Dietz, M. E. (1995). Using portfolios as a framework for professional development. *Journal of Staff Development, 16* (2), 40-43.

Doolittle, P. (1994). Teacher portfolio assessment. [On-line] http://www.ed.gov/databasese/ERIC_Digests/ed385608.html. Retrieved July 10, 2006.

Glatthorn, A. A. (1996). *The teacher's portfolio: Fostering and documenting professional development.* Rockport, MA: ProActive Publications.

Johnson, N., & Rose, L. (1997). *Portfolios: Clarifying, constructing, and enhancing.* Lancaster, PA: Technomic Publishing.

Chapter 1 An Introduction to Your Portfolio

Jones, M., & Shelton, M. (2006). *Developing your portfolio: Enhancing your learning and showing your stuff: A guide for the early childhood student or professional.* New York: Routledge.

Klenowski, V. (2002). *Developing portfolios for learning and assessment: Processes and principles.* London: Routledge Falmer.

Martin, D. B. (1999). *The portfolio planner: Making professional portfolios work for you.* Upper Saddle River, NJ: Prentice Hall.

Rieman, P. L., & Okrasinski, J. (2007). *Creating your teaching portfolio* (2nd ed.). Boston: McGraw Hill.

Tierney, R., Carter, M., & Desai, L. (1991). *Portfolio assessment in the reading-writing classroom*: Norwood, MA: Christopher Gordon.

CHAPTER 2

USING TEACHING STANDARDS TO ORGANIZE YOUR PORTFOLIO

As you plan your portfolio, it is important to organize it in a way that demonstrates your professional growth. Most universities, state departments of education, and national professional organizations have a specified set of standards or goals linked to the practice of effective teaching that may be used as a framework for your portfolio. Standards provide a common language that is understood by professors, peers, or reviewers who may evaluate your work. Regardless of which set of standards you use, all provide a common foundation of knowledge, attitudes, skills, and dispositions that have similar outcomes.

"Using national or state standards when developing a portfolio lends credibility to the document" (Costantino et al., 2006, p. 10). INTASC (Interstate New Teacher Assessment and Support Consortium) standards are often used at universities across the nation for initial certification of teachers because the "National Council for Accreditation for Teacher Education (NCATE) uses the INTASC principles to evaluate teacher education programs" (Rieman & Okrasinski, 2007, p. 30). Furthermore, because the INTASC principles are a core set of expectations for beginning teachers, they are widely applicable, accepted, and used the field (Campbell et al., 2007). The National Association for the Education of Young Children (NAEYC) is the national organization that develops standards for initial licensure for early childhood educators. For these reasons, the Interstate New Teacher Assessment and Support Consortium (INTASC) Principles and the National Association for the Education of Young Children (NAEYC) Core Standards are viable guides to structuring a portfolio for early childhood educators. These standards provide basic understandings about how young children develop and learn and about what competent beginning teachers are able to do.

If you are not using the INTASC principles or the NAEYC standards, a list at the end of the chapter provides web sites for other professional organizations that also contain teaching standards. Any set of these standards could be used to organize your portfolio, as they will all have concepts similar to the INTASC principles and NAEYC standards.

What is INTASC ?

The Interstate New Teacher Assessment and Support Consortium (INTASC) was formed in 1987 to identify what effective teachers should know and should be able to do. The 10 principles, which apply to all P-12 students, serve as tools to demonstrate professional growth and pedagogical knowledge by identifying the knowledge, skills, dispositions, and performances that beginning teachers should possess (http://www.ccsso.org). The consortium is dedicated to the reform of preparation, licensing, and on-going professional development of teachers. More information on INTASC can be found at http://www.ccsso.org/intasc.html. Spend some time reading through the ten INTASC principles and thinking about what each principle means to you.

What are INTASC Principles?

Understanding the process of developing a professional portfolio for early childhood education requires an in-depth understanding of the 10 INTASC principles, the thoughts behind their development, and the impact they have had on the teaching profession. In reading over the actual principles, you will find that all areas that teachers need to develop are included. A list of the INTASC pinciples is found in Figure 2-1. One powerful way to begin working with the INTASC Principles is by asking yourself, "What do teachers do?"

Figure 2-1   Interstate <u>N</u>ew <u>T</u>eachers <u>A</u>ssessment and <u>S</u>upport <u>C</u>onsortium

Principle 1:   **Making content meaningful**
The teacher understands the central concepts, tools of inquiry, and structures of the discipline(s) he or she teaches and creates learning experiences that make these aspects of subject matter meaningful for students.

Principle 2:   **Child development and learning theory**
The teacher understands how children learn and develop and can provide learning opportunities that support their intellectual, social, and personal development.

Principle 3:   **Learning styles/diversity**
The teacher understands how students differ in their approaches to learning and creates instructional opportunities that are adapted to diverse learners.

Principle 4:   **Instructional strategies/problem solving**
The teacher understands and uses a variety of instructional strategies to encourage students' development of critical thinking, problem solving, and performance skills.

Principle 5:   **Motivation and behavior**
The teacher uses an understanding individual and group motivation and behavior to create a learning environment that encourages positive social interaction, active engagements in learning, and self-motivation.

Principle 6:   **Communication/knowledge**
The teacher uses knowledge of effective verbal, nonverbal and media communication techniques to foster active inquiry, collaboration, and supportive interaction in the classroom.

Principle 7:   **Planning for instruction**
The teacher plans instruction based upon knowledge of subject matter, students, the community, and curriculum goals.

Principle 8:   **Assessment**
The teacher understands and uses formal and informal assessment strategies to evaluate and ensure the continuous intellectual, social, and physical development of the learner.

Principle 9:   **Professional growth/reflection**
The teacher is a reflective practitioner who continually evaluates the effects of his or her choices and actions on others (students, parents, and other professionals in the learning community) and who actively seeks out opportunities to grow professionally.

Principle 10:   **Interpersonal relationships**
The teacher fosters relationships with school colleagues, parents, and agencies in the larger community to support students' learning and well-being.

What is NAEYC?

The National Association for the Education of Young Children (NAEYC) is the nation's largest and most influential organization of early childhood educators dedicated solely to enhancing the lives of young children and their families through research, professional journals, conferences, and the development of standards and accreditation. For over 80 years, the organization has worked "to provide the best tools and information about early childhood development" (http://www.naeyc.org/teachers, p. 1) so that all children from birth through age eight who are in child care centers, family day care, homes, and public and private schools will receive a high-quality, developmentally appropriate education. The organization supports children and their families, teachers, and administrators by providing standards for professional preparation, accrediting programs for young children, developing position statements, advocating for excellence in early childhood education, lobbying, engaging in federal legislation, publishing magazines and journals, holding conferences for early childhood educators, and promoting and disseminating research to influence public policy (www.naeyc.org).

What are the NAEYC Core Standards?

1. **Promoting child development and learning**
   Candidates use their understanding of young children's characteristics and needs and of multiple interacting influences of children's development and learning, to create environments that are healthy, respectful, supportive and challenging for all children.
2. **Building family and community relationships**
   Candidates know about, understand, and value the importance and complex characteristics of children's families and communities. They use this understanding to create respectful, reciprocal relationships that support and empower families, and to involve all families in their children's development and learning.
3. **Observing, documenting, and assessing to support young children and families**
   Candidates know about and understand the goals, benefits, and uses of assessment. They know about and use systematic observations, documentation, and other effective assessment strategies in a responsible way, in partnership with families and other professionals, to positively influence children's development and learning.
4. **Teaching and learning**
   Candidates integrate their understanding of and relationships with children and families; their understanding of developmentally effective approaches to teaching and learning, and their knowledge of academic disciplines, to design, implement, and evaluate experiences that promote positive development and learning for all children.
   4a.   Connecting with children and families.
          Candidates know, understand, and use positive relationships and supportive interactions as the foundation for their work with young children.
   4b.   Using developmentally effective approaches
          Candidates know, understand, and use a wide array of effective approaches, strategies, and tools to positively influence young children's development and learning.
   4c.   Understand content knowledge in early education
          Candidates understand the importance of each content area in young children's learning. They know the essential concepts, inquiry tools, and structure of content areas including academic subjects and can identify resources to deepen their understanding.

4d.   Building meaningful curriculum
Candidates use their own knowledge and other resources to design, implement, and evaluate meaningful, challenging curriculum that promotes comprehensive developmental and learning outcomes for all young children.

5. Growing as a professional

Candidates identify and conduct themselves as members of the early childhood profession.

They know and use ethical guidelines and other professional standards related to early childhood practice. They are continuous, collaborative learners who demonstrate knowledgeable, reflective, and critical perspectives on their work, making informed decisions that integrate knowledge from a variety of sources. They are informed advocates for sound educational practices and policies (www.naeyc.org).

Figure 2-2 provides a cross-reference of correlates the INTASC principles with the NAEYC Core Standards. The correlation between these two sets of standards may be a helpful tool as you continue to develop your portfolio.

Figure 2-2   Cross-Reference Chart of NAEYC Initial Licensure Standards and INTASC Principles

NAEYC Initial Licensure Standards	INTASC Performance Principles									
	#1	#2	#3	#4	#5	#6	#7	#8	#9	#10
1. Promoting child development and learning		X	X		X		X			
2. Building family and community relationships			X				X			X
3. Observing, documenting, and assessing to support young children and families				X			X	X		
4. Teaching and learning										
4a. Connecting with children and families						X	X			X
4b. Using developmentally effective approaches	X	X	X	X	X	X	X			
4c. Understanding content knowledge in early education	X									
4d. Building meaningful curriculum	X	X		X	X		X			
5. Becoming a professional									X	X

You have learned that INTASC principles and NAEYC standards are often used to demonstrate what a beginning early childhood teacher should know and do to be effective in an early childhood classroom. You have also seen how the two sets of standards are interrelated. Now, you are ready to put this knowledge to work.

Activity 2-1   Linking Artifacts to the Standards

Step One: Take the time to generate a list of the activities an early childhood educator does throughout the school day. Items on your list probably include writing lesson plans, teaching various subjects, conferencing with parents, mediating classroom disputes, nursing wounds, motivating learners, and more. The list is endless and unique to each individual teacher and school setting.

Step Two: Using the list you created, how could you verify your proficiency in each item? You may say you can write a good lesson plan, but how can this be proven? The answer is through a well-designed, organized artifact. What goes into your portfolio is the "proof" that you are a competent teacher. That concrete, tangible evidence is referred to as an artifact. The list that you generated in Step 1 is probably a list of artifacts. Artifacts are simply pieces of evidence that exhibit what you know about teaching and learning. (Artifacts will be defined and examined more closely in Chapter 4.) Figure 2-3 shows how a specific activity can become a portfolio artifact. Follow the example provided below and develop a possible artifact for each activity you listed in Step 1.

Figure 2-3   Artifact Activity

Activity	Artifact	Other Possible Artifacts
Lesson Plans	A detailed, well-written plan	
Teaching Subject Matter	Supervisor's evaluation Self-evaluation Photographs of you teaching	
Conferencing with Parents	Letters Notes Emails to parents Parent conferences Behavior plan of action	
Mediating Dispute	Classroom rules and procedures Letters to students and their families Classroom Management Plan	
Nursing Wounds	Injury Policies and Procedures Plan Reassuring songs or actions Self-reflection	
Motivating Learners	Lesson plans Classroom reward system Lesson motivators Classroom layout plan	

Step Three: Think about the INTASC principle under which each teacher activity and artifact would best fit. For example, a lesson plan could demonstrate your ability to make content meaningful. This would then demonstrate your knowledge of INTASC Principle #1. A lesson plan could also motivate young children. Then your artifact could be placed under INTASC Principle #5. Some examples of writing ideas for artifacts that match a given activity, and identifying a possible INTASC principle are detailed in Figure 2-4.

Figure 2-4   Identifying Artifacts and Related INTASC Principle

Activity	Artifact	INTASC Principle
Lesson Plans	A detailed, well-written plan	Principles #1-10 Lesson plans should be evident within each INTASC standard to document various aspects of a lesson (planning, teaching, assessment).
Teaching Subject Matter	Supervisor's evaluation Self-evaluation Photographs of you teaching	Principle #1 Lesson plans should be based on standards and curriculum.
Conferencing with Parents	Letters Notes Emails to parents Parent conferences Behavior plan of action	Principle #10 Interpersonal relationships
Mediating Dispute	Classroom rules and procedures Letters to students and their families Classroom Management Plan	Principle #5 Motivation and classroom management
Nursing Wounds	Injury Policies and Procedures Plan Reassuring songs or actions Self-reflection	Principle #4 The teacher understands a variety of teaching strategies to encourage students' thinking and performance skills.
Motivating Learners	Lesson plans Classroom reward system Lesson motivators Classroom layout plan	Principle #5 Motivation and classroom management

Step Four: Figure 2-5 asks you to read each activity and artifact and decide under which INTASC principle you would place them. The first one is completely done for you. You created a dramatic play center in a classroom. To document that event, you made a brochure for parents explaining the learning objectives for a play center. Then you decided that this artifact fit nicely under INTASC Principle #2 because play is an important format in children's development, and you can document that through various learning theories. The second activity involves planning a folk tale study. Your artifact is a list of 10 folk tales from many countries. Write the INTASC principle under which you would place this artifact. Complete the next two entries by adding the INTASC principle under which you would place each item. Then, add some of your own activities and complete the chart. Another way to process this information might be to create a table similar Figure 2-5 using your course syllabi to decide if any of your class assignments could be viable artifacts; then align your course assignments with the INTASC principles.

Figure 2-5   Using Activities to Identify Artifacts and INTASC Principles

Activity	Artifact	INTASC Principle
Create a dramatic play center	Brochure including pictures to parents explaining the learning objectives of the center	INTASC Principle #2 Child Development and Learning Theory
Plan a folk tale study	List 10 books that are folk tales from various cultures.	
Attend a professional development meeting	Reflection paper on what went on at a State Conference for Professional Development Schools	
Write a newsletter to parents	A newsletter that illustrates written communication	

Summary

This chapter explains the importance of and the rationale for using standards as a way to organize your portfolio. If you are an early childhood educator, we recommend that you use NAEYC standards. Your school may very well expect you to use a specific set of standards as a framework for your portfolio. Many colleges require students to use INTASC principles because portfolio can be a part of the NCATE accreditation process. In that case, you may want to use two sets of standards and cross-reference them like was done in Figure 2-2. However, if you have the option to choose a set of standards as an organizational framework, usually the performance outcomes are similar and involve five universal themes:

- Knowledge of content, subject matter, and educational theory
- Planning, delivery, and assessment of instruction
- Classroom organization and management
- Human relationships with children and adults
- Professionalism (Costantino et al., 2006)

Suggested Web Sites

American Association of Colleges for Teacher Education (AACTE), http://www.aacte.org
Association of Teacher Educators (ATE), http://www.ate1.org
Association for Childhood Education International (ACEI), http://www.udel.edu/bateman/acei/
Council for Exceptional Children (CEC), www.ced.sped.org
Council of Chief State School Officers (CCSSO), http://www.ccsso.org
National Association for the Education of Young Children, www.naeyc.org
National Association of State Boards of Education (NASBE), http: www.nasbe.org.
National Board for Professional Teaching Standards (NBPTS), http://www.nbpts.org/
National Education Association (NEA), http:///www.nea.org/
Teacher Work Sample (TWS), http://www.uni.edu/itq/RTWS/index.htm;
www.suu.edu/faculty/harrisg/tws/

References

Campbell, D. M., Cignetti, P. B., Melenyzer, B. J., Nettles, D. H., & Wyman, R. M. (2007). *How to develop a professional portfolio: A manual for teachers* (4th ed.). Boston: Allyn & Bacon.

Costantino, P. M., De Lorenzo, M. N., & Kobrinski, E. J. (2006). *Developing a professional teaching portfolio: A guide for success* (2nd ed.). Boston: Allyn & Bacon.

Rieman, P. L., & Okrasinski, J. (2007). *Creating your teaching portfolio* (2nd ed.). New York: McGraw Hill.

CHAPTER 3

SETTING UP YOUR PORTFOLIO

Portfolios are publications, like books and magazines. The more appealing they are, the better chance they have of being read and taken seriously (Jones & Shelton, 2006). To be effective, your portfolio needs to have a well-established organizational system that makes sense to you, and that you can explain to other educators. You already know that a portfolio in early childhood education will be organized around standards that are used by your university and that represent your understanding of young children's development. In this book, we use the Interstate New Teacher Assessment and Support Consortium (INTASC) Principles because these are the principles required by the National Council for the Accreditation of Teacher Education (NCATE) for accreditation. "NCATE accreditation is a mark of distinction and provides recognition that the college of Education has met national professional standards for the preparation of teachers" (www.ccsso.org/intasc.html). We also use the National Association for the Education of Young Children (NAEYC) Standards because these are the standards that govern our field of early childhood education (www.naeyc.org).

Traditional portfolios are those that are published on paper, but a recent advancement in the field of portfolio development is the electronic portfolio, which will be discussed more fully in Chapter 5. With either type of portfolio, the organization will be similar. "Traditional portfolios are simpler to use when you wish to display hard copies of certain artifacts or create smaller portable portfolios, [but] in terms of organization and storage, the accumulation of all your artifacts can quickly become . . . unwieldy" (Rieman & Okrasinski, 2007, p. 25). In addition to portfolio development, electronic portfolios also require multimedia expertise.

Organization of the Traditional Paper Portfolio
A traditional paper portfolio is usually contained in an extra wide or extended 3-inch three-ring binder, preferably in white, black or blue. Extra-wide dividers designate each section, to assist with management. To access materials within each section, extra-wide tabs should be used. These, like the extended binder and dividers, can be purchased at most office supply stores or on-line. Artifacts should be contained in plastic sheet protectors.

Outside and Inside Cover Pages The portfolio should be personalized with an "outside cover page" and an "inside cover page," that both include the title, your (the preparer's) name, your major, your college, and your university (see Figure 3-1).

Figure 3-1   Outside and Inside Cover Page

PROFESSIONAL PORTFOLIO

EARLY CHILDHOOD EDUCATION

XYZ UNIVERSITY

YOUR NAME

Table of Contents As in any book, the Table of Contents organizes the evidence you wish to display. The Table of Contents should be a directory of all the documents that are included in your portfolio, listed in the order in which they appear. For example, under INTASC I: Knowledge of Subject Matter, you would list all artifacts in the order in which they appear. It is wise to avoid numbering items or pages because the artifacts may be constantly changing (see Figure 3-2).

Philosophy Statement Following the Table of Contents, you will lay the foundation for your portfolio with a thoughtful, well-written philosophy statement. Your philosophy statement is a concise, well-written statement that details your beliefs and values related to teaching, learning, and young children. It represents you and the ideals to which you aspire, connecting theory to practice. Chapter 6 looks more carefully at your personal and professional educational philosophy, and includes examples of excellent philosophy statements written by college students.

The portfolio is divided into three main sections: Section I: Personal Background; Section II: Professional Background; and Section III: Appendix. Each section should begin with a page that identifies that portion of the portfolio.

Section I: Personal Background

As you can see from Figure 3-2, the personal background section provides a glimpse of who you as a pre-service teacher, and offers a profile of your background and experiences. You should ask: Who am I? What is important for others to know about me? What experiences have I had that will demonstrate my readiness to teach? Usually this section also contains an autobiography, a resume, college transcripts, other vital statistics, references, certificates, certifications, and supporting documents.

The personal background section often begins with an autobiography—a 2 -3 page "story" of you as a pre-service teacher. Include something about yourself, your family background, your interests and hobbies. The most important part of the story comprises why you decided to become an educator of young children. What qualities do you possess that will enhance your qualifications as a teacher? What were some early experiences that influenced why you want to teach and how you plan to teach? What are some central ideas about teaching and learning that will influence your development as an emerging teacher?

Figure 3-2   Table of Contents

Table of Contents

I. Personal Background

- Acceptance letter to the University
- Official Transcript from the University
- Praxis I Test Scores
- Acceptance letter to the Early Childhood Education Program
- Autobiography
- Philosophy of Education
- Dean's List Letters
- Kappa Delta Pi Certificate
- Criminal Background Clearance
- Resume

II. Professional Background

➢ INTASC Principle 1-The teacher understands the central concepts, tools of inquiry, and structures of the disciplines he or she teaches and can create learning experiences that make these aspects of the subject matter meaningful for students.
- Dramatic Play Box
- Math Lesson Plan on Measurement
- Annotated Book List

➢ INTASC Principle 2-The teacher understands how children learn and develop and can provide learning opportunities that support their intellectual, social, and personal development.
- Observation Report
- Child Observation Study
- Toddler Observation Study

➢ INTASC Principle 3-The teacher understands how students differ in their approaches to learning and creates instructional opportunities that are adapted to diverse learners.
- Special Education Observation Report
- Child Case Study
- Hyperlexia Research Paper

➢ INTASC Principle 4- The teacher understands and uses a variety of instructional strategies to encourage students' development of critical thinking, problem solving, and performance skills.
- Phonemic Awareness Lesson Plan
- Science 5-E Lesson Plan on Weather
- Post Office Writing Center

Figure 3-2   Table of Contents, continued

➤ INTASC Principle 5-The teacher uses an understanding individual and group motivation and behavior to create a learning environment that encourages positive social interaction, active engagements in learning, and self-motivation.
- Kinesiology Fitness Lesson Plan
- Interest Inventory
- Ice Cream Cone Behavior Management Plan

➤ INTASC Principle 6-The teacher uses knowledge of effective verbal, nonverbal and media communication techniques to foster active inquiry, collaboration, and supportive interaction in the classroom.
- Technology NETS List
- Multimedia Lesson Plan and PowerPoint Project
- *The Library* comprehension Lesson Plan using technology

➤ INTASC Principle 7-The teacher plans instruction based upon knowledge of subject matter, students, the community, and curriculum goals.
- Curriculum Web
- Comprehension Lesson Plan
- Thematic Book Unit

➤ INTASC Principle 8-The teacher understands and uses formal and informal assessment strategies to evaluate and ensure the continuous intellectual, social, and physical development of the learner.
- Cycle of Learning Lesson Plan on Families
- 2-Day Cycle of Learning Plan on Units of Weight
- Phonological Awareness Project
- 3-Day Cycle of Learning Lesson Plan

➤ INTASC Principle 9-The teacher is a reflective practitioner who continually evaluates the effects of his or her choices and actions on others (students, parents, and other professionals in the learning community) and who actively seeks out opportunities to grow professionally.
- Code of Ethical Conduct Case Plan
- Persuasive Essay: Kindergarten Naps
- Multicultural Day Reflection
- Comics in the Classroom Project

➤ INTASC Principle 10-The teacher fosters relationships with school colleagues, parents, and agencies in the larger community to support students' learning and well-being.
- Samples of Letter Writing
  1. Field Trip Letter
  2. Letter of Referral
  3. Letter of Thanks

• Summary of Interview with a Preschool Teacher

Figure 3-2   Table of Contents, continued

• Family Literacy Bag

III. Appendix
- Picture from Volunteering at Ridge Ruxton School
- Pictures from Pre-School Field Placement
- Mentor Teacher Evaluation
- Primary Internship Evaluation
- Pictures from Primary Student Teaching Placement
- Attendance Certificate from at a Professional Convention
- Student Teaching Primary Placement Evaluation from Mentor and University Supervisor

Other items that might be included in the Personal Background Section could include:

Letter of Introduction
Resume
University Transcript(s) from all higher education institutions attended
PRAXIS I and II Scores
Speech and Hearing Screening results
Letter of Acceptance into an Early Childhood Education Program or other program
Letters of Recommendations
Work Experience Documents
Honors, Awards, or Special Recognition
Membership Certificates or Cards
Certificates of Participation in Workshops or Conferences
Documentation of any Special Skill
Documentation of Volunteer Work

This list is not intended to be complete, and you may have additional items that you want to incorporate.

Section II: Professional Background

This section is the heart and soul of the portfolio! This is where your portfolio becomes a true professional document and not a scrapbook because it contains a record of quantitative and qualitative growth over time under each standard. Section II provides artifacts that evidence your knowledge of professional standards and reflects your growth and development. This section of artifacts actually helps you better understand teaching as a profession, gain greater self-understanding, and capture the complexities of teaching.

Following the Section II identification page, there should be a complete list of the ten Interstate New Teacher Assessment and Support Consortium (INTASC) Principles, written in their entirety, followed by a complete version of the National Association for the Education of Young Children (NAEYC) Standards. If you are using another set of standards, it is recommended that they, too, be listed in their entirety. Each of the ten INTASC Principles or defining standards being used should have its own title page and corresponding labeled tab, as these are the main subheadings in Section II. If you are using two sets of standards, we recommend including the corresponding standard on the title page as well. Since our university uses INTASC and NAEYC Standards for Early Childhood Education majors, each title page should include the INTASC Principle, written in its entirety, as well as the corresponding NAEYC Standard(s). See Figure 3-3 for a sample standard title page.

Figure 3-3   Standard Title Page using INTASC and NAEYC Standards

INTASC Principle 1:
Knowledge of Subject Matter

The teacher understands the central concepts, tools of inquiry, and structures of the discipline(s) he or she teaches, and creates learning experiences that make these aspects of subject matter meaningful for students.

NAEYC Standards

4b. Using developmentally effective approaches

4c.Understanding content knowledge in early education

4d. Building meaningful curriculum

The artifacts that support the identified INTASC principle and NAEYC standard(s) follow the cover page. Artifacts, while discussed in more detail in Chapter 4, should be varied and can include many of the items in this list of potential artifacts. The checklist below allows you to keep track of the artifacts that you have selected for use in your portfolio.

Table 3-1   Potential Artifacts for Section II of Your Portfolio

ARTIFACT	Completed/Provided
Activity Ideas	
Adaptations of Materials or Instruction	
Annotated Bibliographies	
Assessment Instruments (Formal and Informal)	
Assessment Strategies	
Audiotapes	
Bulletin Board Creations	
Case Studies/ Child Studies	
Checklists	
Classroom Designs	
Classroom Management Plans	
Displays	
Diversity Ideas	
Exhibits	
Field Trip Ideas and Experiences	
Flannel Board Ideas	
Interactions with Children, Demonstrated on Video	
Instructional Strategies, Materials, Designs, Activities	
Interviews with Parents, Teachers, Specialists, Administrators	
Journal Entries	
Learning Centers	
Lesson Plans	
Letters to Parents, Colleagues, Community Workers	
List of Services and Resources for Students and Teachers	
Literature for Children	
Logs	
Meetings	
Music Ideas and Activities	
Newsletters	
Observation Reports	
Observation Tools	
Reactions to Newspaper Articles/Reports	
Personal/Professional Assessment	
Philosophy Paper/Statement	
Photographs	
Play: Value, Ideas, and Integration	

Posters Created

Table 3-1   Potential Artifacts for Section II of Your Portfolio, continued

ARTIFACT	Completed/Provided
PowerPoint Presentations	
Presentations	
Professional Development	
Professional Literature	
Puppets	
Prop Boxes	
References	
Research Papers and Reports	
Resource Files and Lists	
Self-Evaluations	
Service-Learning Projects	
Simulations	
Software Programs, Evaluations, or Lists of Developmentally Appropriate Practice	
Students' Work Samples	
Teacher Evaluations	
Technology Review/Competencies	
Testimonies	
Thematic Units	
Transition Ideas	
Videotape Critiques and Ideas	
Volunteer Work and Experiences	
Web Sites	
Written Test	

This is not a complete list of artifacts. All pre-service teachers will have many and varied experiences and can provide artifacts that have impacted their learning.

Table 3-2   Possible Artifacts for INTASC Principles and NAEYC Standards

INTASC Principles and NAEYC Standards	Possible Artifacts That Can Support Different Competencies

INTASC 1 Subject Matter
NAEYC Standards
  4b. Using developmentally effective approaches
  4c. Understanding content knowledge in early education
  4d. Building meaningful curriculum
	Lesson plans; Videotaped lessons; Unit plans; Student work; Individualized materials; Curriculum plans; Projects; Photographs; Connections to national, state, and local standards; Instruction focused on key ideas.

INTASC 2 Knowledge of human development
NAEYC Standards
  1. Promoting child development and learning
  4b. Using developmental effective approaches
  4d. Building meaningful curriculum
	Bulletin board ideas; Essays; Observation reports; Child Study; Case Study; Lesson Plans; Teacher-made materials; Projects; Developmental profiles; Checklists; Student Portfolio; Letters to Parents; Student work samples; Papers documenting typical or atypical development; Instruction designed to meet learners' needs based on age, socioeconomic status, development, learning style, readiness, ability, culture, social group, and/or values.

INTASC 3 Instruction adapted for diverse learners
NAEYC Standards
  1. Promoting child development and learning
  2. Building family and community relationships
  4b. Using developmentally effective approaches
	Lesson plans (evidence of variety of strategies); Services and resources for diverse learners; Interviews with specialists; Individualized Education Plans; Literature reviews; Special education reports; Analysis of Assessments; Annotated bibliographies; Differentiation of instruction; Student work samples.

INTASC 4 Use of multiple strategies and resources
NAEYC Standards
  4b. Using developmentally effective approaches
  4d. Building meaningful curriculum
	Lesson plans; Curriculum plans; Evaluations; Peer critiques; Observation reports; Thematic units; Projects; Pictures; Videotapes; Materials; Reflections; Student work samples; Evidence of a variety of instructional strategies; Instruction encouraging critical thinking and problem solving.

Table 3-2   Possible Artifacts for INTASC Principles and NAEYC Standards,
              continued

INTASC Principles and NAEYC Standards	Possible Artifacts That Can Support Different Competencies
INTASC 5 Learning environment/motivation and behavior NAEYC Standards 1. Promoting child development and learning 3. Observing, documenting, and assessing to support young children and families 4b. Using developmentally effective approaches 4d. Building meaningful curriculum	Classroom Management plans; Cooperative learning strategies; Field trip plans; Activities; Ideas; Journal entries; Case Studies; Assessments; Observation reports; Lesson plans; Student portfolios; Unit plans; Classroom designs; Students' work samples; Using time effectively; Teacher-made materials; Evidence of positive, productive learning environment; Engaging students in active learning; Collaboration with team members, parents, administrators to promote positive behavior.
INTASC 6 Effective Communication and Technology NAEYC Standards 4a. Connecting with children and families 4b. Using developmentally effective approaches	Lesson plans (technology focus); Family theme bags; Projects; Media/technology activities; Research papers; Lesson plans; Newsletters; Computer programs; Media evaluation; Software selection/evaluation; Demonstration of professional use of oral and/or written language skills; Integrating instructional technology; Using technology to meet professional needs; Student work samples.
INTASC 7 Planning for Instruction NAEYC Standards 1. Promoting child development and learning 2. Building family and community relationships 3. Observing, documenting, and assessing to support young children and families 4a. Connecting with children and families 4b. Using developmentally effective approaches 4d. Building meaningful curriculum	Lesson plans; Evidence of modification; Photographs; Student work samples; Outlines of instructional planning; Short- and long-term objectives and planning; Pacing guides; Teacher-made materials; Unit plans; Observation reports; Case studies; Aligning objectives to national, state, and local curriculum; Addressing students' needs and strengths; Using data to adjust instruction.

Table 3-2   Possible Artifacts for INTASC Principles and NAEYC Standards,
            continued

INTASC Principles and NAEYC Standards	Possible Artifacts That Can Support Different Competencies
INTASC 8 Assessment of student learning NAEYC Standard 3. Observing, documenting, and assessing to support young children and families	Assessments (formal and informal); Case studies; Projects; Interviews with students; Evaluations and critiques of assessments; Cycle of learning; Student work and assessment samples; Using assessment to demonstrate positive impact on learning; Assessment plan; Use of pre- and post-assessments; Use of formative assessments; Demonstrate ability to diagnose, monitor, and document student progress; Modify instruction based on assessment results.
INTASC 9 Professional growth and reflection NAEYC Standards 5. Becoming a professional	Progress reports; Reflection statements; Review of Code of Ethics; Videotaped lessons and critiques; Professional memberships; Presentations; Attendance at workshops and conferences; Self-assessments; Consultation of professional literature; Evidence of positive impact of professional development on student achievement; Classroom observations and data analysis to evaluate outcomes and revise practice.
INTASC 10. Interpersonal relationships NAEYC Standards 2. Building family and community relationships 4a. Connecting with children and families 5. Becoming a professional	Community resources; Collegial activities to improve teaching and learning; Effective communication with families; Field trip plans; Identification and use of community resources to foster student learning; Letters to parents; Community exploration; Interviews; Volunteer experiences; Newsletters; Service-learning projects;

Section III: Appendix

The Appendix is a collection of supplementary materials that are valued by you but are not related directly to an identified competency or standard. For clarity, items in the appendix should be supported by a caption. These items do not need to be accompanied by a reflective narrative. These items could include photographs, lengthy papers, letters from parents, and memorabilia that is not closely linked to a specific artifact. A list of the items in the Appendix should appear in the Table of Contents in the order in which they appear.

Activity 3-1

Refer back to Table 3-1. From this list, identify items from your course work that could be considered portfolio artifacts. Use Table 3-2 to correlate your artifacts to the INTASC Standards. Figure 3-4 illustrates an Evidence and Standards Cross-Reference Chart (Costantino et al., 2006), which you could also use to document how you are connecting standards to the content in your portfolio. You might include one of these organizational formats in your portfolio, as it clearly delineates the relationship between the standards and your evidence.

Figure 3-4   Evidence and Standard Cross-Reference Chart

Portfolio Evidence	INTASC Principles									
	#1	#2	#3	#4	#5	#6	#7	#8	#9	#10
Family Theme Bag			X			X				
Field Trip Plan							X			X
Lesson Plan: Phonemic Awareness	X			X		X	X	X		
Behavior Management Plan					X					
Philosophy of Education	X	X							X	
Integrated Thematic Unit	X	X	X	X	X	X	X	X		

Adapted from Costantino et al., 2006

Summary

The organization of the portfolio is critical to the management and the accessibility of artifacts and documents. While you decide which artifact you include in the portfolio, they should be organized in a commonsensical way. Using three main sections is a logical way to organize items. Artifacts that tell "who you are" are placed in the Personal Section; items that show "what you know and have learned" are located in the Professional Section, and supporting items of interest are placed in the Appendix.

Suggested Web Sites

Portfolio guidelines from various Colleges of Education can be found at these web sites:
- College of Education @ MU: Portfolio
  http://education.missouri.edu/TDP/_TDP/students/portfolio.php
- University of Central Florida – College of Education
  http://reach.ucf.edu/~ed_found/gpi.html
- College of Education | Idaho State University
  http://ed.isu.edu/assessments/asItpa.shtml

References

Costantino, P. M., De Lorenzo, M. N., & Kobrinski, E. J. (2006). *Developing a professional teaching portfolio: A guide for success* (2nd ed.). Boston, MA: Allyn & Bacon.

Interstate New Teacher Assessment and Support Consortium (1992). *Model standards for beginning teacher licensing, assessment and development: A resource for state dialogue.* [On-line] www.ccsso.org. Retrieved May 23, 2007.

Jones, M., & Shelton, M. (2006). *Developing your portfolio: Enhancing your learning and showing your stuff: A guide for the early childhood student or professional.* New York: Routledge.

National Association for the Education of Young Children. (2007). *National Association for the Education of Young Children—Promoting excellence in early childhood education.* [On-line] http://www.naeyc.org/. Retrieved January 24, 2007.

CHAPTER 4

IDENTIFYING ARTIFACTS

The American Heritage Dictionary (3rd ed, 1992) defines "artifact" as "an object produced or shaped by human craft, especially a tool, a weapon, or an ornament of archaeological or historical interest" (p.105). Thinking about artifacts in this way, the items you choose for your portfolio are exhibits that showcase what you know about teaching and learning. The pieces of evidence that make up your portfolio are shaped by you into a useful tool that documents and assesses your skills to date and helps others understand you as an emerging early childhood professional. You may include any item that you feel helps illustrate your abilities in meeting the portfolio criteria established by your school. While you are in the collecting and developmental stages, we recommend that you save a variety of artifacts, even if they are not necessarily representative of your "best" work. While "best work" portfolios are preferred by some, others see a value in selecting some work that may not exemplify best practices. For example, perhaps you tried out a lesson that was unsuccessful. Did you learn from it? Of course you did. So you might want to include one not so successful lesson and explain what you would do differently if you were to try it again. Your reflective narrative might sound like this:

> I wrote and implemented a lesson plan on reading comprehension to second graders. I focused on reading a story and sequencing the events of the story. During the lesson, students listened to the story on a cassette tape and then participated in a class discussion about sequencing. The students then engaged in guided practice and independent practice by completing an assessment. My assessment results showed that I needed to re-teach the lesson. Therefore, I had to think critically about how to improve my future lesson. I realized that had I modeled my expectations and used sequencing as an active group activity, my students would have had a better understanding of sequencing. In my re-teaching, I incorporated both of these methods. Assessment results the second time were much more successful.

These kinds of artifacts provide an authentic picture of your strengths and areas of need. They allow you to set goals for self-improvement. Some authorities on portfolio suggest that even the final showcase portfolio include evidence of both strengths and weaknesses (Burke, 1999); however, most feel that your Interview Portfolio should represent only your best work (Antonek et al., 1977; Costantino et al., 2006).

Artifacts describe what you know and what you can do (Jones & Shelton, 2006). You can include paper documents, electronic documents, electronic images, audio and videotapes. Artifacts for interns could include field experiences, lesson plans, units of teaching, field trip plans, case studies, service-learning projects, assessment strategies, action research projects, classroom management plans, parent projects, journals, reflections, work samples, photographs, technological projects, article reviews, diagnostic evaluation plans, diagnostic reports, annotated book lists, observations, interviews with teachers and/or children, communications with parents, self-evaluations, papers on various abilities or disabilities, and community service activities. Other potential artifacts are listed in Table 3-2. Many of the assignments in your professional courses and internship experiences are appropriate as potential artifacts. Refer to Figure 3-4 to provide you with ideas for artifacts in various types of professional courses.

Choosing Appropriate Artifacts

How you select artifacts for your portfolio depends on your stage of development and the purpose of your portfolio. If you are in the collection or development stages, you will want to collect a wide range of many and diverse artifacts, but if you are refining materials for a showcase or interview portfolio, your task changes. In the beginning you are selecting the best evidence you have that documents your competencies in the many areas being assessed. Answering the questions posed by Costantino et al. (2006) will help you determine whether or not the document is worthy of inclusion.

- Does the evidence align with the purpose of your portfolio?
- Does the evidence support a performance standard or theme?
- Is the evidence credible and does it support progress toward your professional growth, learning, and goals?
- Is the evidence an item that provides substance and meaning to your portfolio?
- If this evidence were eliminated, would it detract from the credibility of your portfolio? (p. 32)

The INTASC Principles, NAEYC Standards, or other standards are used as criteria and the framework for portfolio in early childhood education, but the standards and the indicators for each must be demonstrated. One way to do this is by creating or charting collected evidence on a grid. Table 3-2 provides possible artifacts that support each INTASC Principle and corresponding NAEYC Standard, and Figure 4-1 provides sample artifacts from courses that are probably taught in most early childhood programs. Both tools could be adapted to any criteria. Figure 4-2 is a grid for charting the evidence you have collected using INTASC principles and NAEYC Standards.

Which Artifacts are Best for My Portfolio?

Once again, only you can decide which artifacts are best for your portfolio, with suggestions from your professors, instructors, and peers. Selection of items depends on the purpose and the type of portfolio. We highly recommend that in your final showcase and interview portfolios that the indicators for each standard be met fully, and that each principle contain approximately the same number of artifacts—usually three to five. These artifacts, while self-selected, should represent your expertise in all areas expected of early childhood teachers:

- Knowledge of early childhood content
- In-depth knowledge of child development
- Ability to plan, execute, and assess meaningful learning experiences for all children
- Opportunities to promote and support every child's maximal development
- Understanding developmentally appropriate practice
- Use of formal and informal assessment
- Use of a variety of instructional strategies to encourage higher other thinking skills
- Use of diagnostic, summative, and formative assessment

• Ability to foster motivation, positive social interactions, and active learning
• Ability to create a safe and culturally responsive environment
• Ability to build family and community relationships
• Ability to foster effective communication techniques.
• Ability to form relationships with school colleagues, administrators, families and the community.
• Ability to reflect and self-evaluate as a practitioner.
• Desire to continue to grow as a professional.

Figure 4-1   Sample Artifacts from Early Childhood Courses

Course Description	Sample Artifacts That Might Be Appropriate for Your Portfolio
Introduction to Early Childhood Education or any beginning level course where portfolio is introduced	Autobiographical paper Theorist research paper Paper on problems and trends in early childhood education Article reflections or critiques Observation in early childhood settings Philosophy statement Newsletter to parents or families
Any child development course	Case studies Article reflections or critiques Report on stages of development (infant, toddler, preK, kindergarten, Grade 1, 2, and 3) Report or paper on types of development (social, emotional, cognitive, physical, literacy) Paper or presentation on developmental theorists (Piaget, Vygotsky, Erikson, Freud, Gesell, Gardner, Maslow, and others) Paper on atypical development
Introduction to Special Education course	Report on an IEP meeting Paper on the characteristics of exceptionalities Observation in an inclusive environment Adaptive strategies report or demonstration Paper that documents understanding of the laws and litigation
Any course geared to infant development	Field observations at an infant center Field observations at a shelter Community service project in a shelter Parenting newsletter Report on Head Start Investigative piece on services and resources for families
Any course that addresses teaching in a multicultural, multiethnic society	Interview with someone from a culture different from your own Share an object that reflects your own culture Community service project Make a list of stereotypical items found in a classroom

Figure 4-1 Sample Artifacts from Early Childhood Courses, continued

Course Description	Sample Artifacts That Might Be Appropriate for Your Portfolio
Any course that addresses issues of interactive technology and early childhood education	Early childhood software review/critique Observations of children using technology Review and analysis of web sites appropriate for young children Using a PowerPoint presentation in the classroom Electronic portfolios Using technology to enhance your resume Multimedia presentation
Reading course aimed at studying theories, processes, and acquisition of reading and language arts, including cognitive, linguistic, social, and physiological factors involved in oral and written language development	Research project on reading/writing Literacy acquisition study Memory retrieval test Issues in literacy paper Writing sample analysis Article critique on phonics Presentation/paper on theorists in the field of reading/language arts
Any course on advanced writing for early childhood majors	Resume Parent newsletter Letter of recommendation for a student A letter of referral Reflective journal writings
Any curriculum courses involving best practices in curriculum and methods of teaching children between 4-6 years of age	Ethic/moral dilemma paper using NAEYC Code of Ethics Letter of introduction to field placement mentor teacher Reflective journal writing Attendance/report on a non-teaching school event Lesson plans A center activity plan Dramatic play prop box Integrated web Integrated unit Project involving families Revise Philosophy Statement
Emergent literacy course that examines strategies, materials, and experiences for literacy development in children birth to age 5	Word story activity to be taught and critiqued Lesson plans in phonemic awareness, phonics, vocabulary development, comprehension, and fluency Family literacy bag Shared reading lesson Phonemic awareness lesson A lesson involving rhyming words Read-aloud lesson Design a literacy center Evaluation of PreK and Kindergarten literacy programs

Figure 4-1   Sample Artifacts from Early Childhood Courses, continued

Course Description	Sample Artifacts That Might Be Appropriate for Your Portfolio
One course or multiple courses that address the teaching and integration of the arts (music, drama, dance, movement, art) for young children	Lesson plan using the arts to teach a prereading activity Design centers incorporating the arts Teach and reflect on a movement activity done in your field placement Draw-a-story activity
Any course in science methods that familiarizes students with appropriate content, methods, materials and evaluation of teaching science to the young child	A case study documenting science learning in the classroom Plan and execute a lesson that analyzes data, forms generalizations about the data, and applies the explanation to another situation or problem. Design a hands-on science center Design a science lesson that integrates another content area
Mathematics methods in early childhood education	Design a math game Plan, execute, and assess a math lesson in your placement Create a chart or graph that illustrates and organizes data
Methods for identifying and assessing disabilities in early childhood education	Attend an IEP meeting Use the Developmental Activities Screening Inventory (DASI) to assess a child Write a recommendation to parents for intervention strategies for a child identified with a disability Paper on a specific disability
A course that examines and uses a range of literacy and reading assessments and that focuses on the relationship of assessment to instructional planning for diverse learners	Use miscue analysis on a child to detect reading strengths and weaknesses Reading and writing sample analysis Analyze the results for the Motivation to Read survey Running records
A course on teaching reading in the primary grades (1-3) with emphasis on best practices, research, materials, and developmentally appropriate active learning related to the process of learning to read	Child literacy study Plan, execute, and assess a directed reading lesson Plan, execute, and assess an guided reading lesson Plan, execute, and assess a fluency lesson Plan, execute, and assess a vocabulary lesson Plan, execute, and assess a phonics lesson Plan, execute, and assess a comprehension lesson Plan, execute, and assess a phonemic awareness lesson Running records to evaluate a child's reading

Figure 4-1   Sample Artifacts from Early Childhood Courses, continued

Course Description	Sample Artifacts That Might Be Appropriate for Your Portfolio
One or more methods courses that look at developmentally appropriate objectives, materials, lesson plans, activities, methods, and assessments for teaching all content areas (science, social studies, language arts, and mathematics) in grades 1-3	Plan, execute, and assess one lesson in every content area Field trip plan Videotaping of your teaching with reflection & critique Peer observation/critique Service-learning project Classroom management plan Cycle of learning (2 concurrent lessons using pre- and post-assessments) Journal reflections Interview your mentor teacher about the profession
The final student teaching experience involving 16 weeks in a public school	Write daily lesson plans Evaluations and assessment of students (informal, formal) Attend IEP meetings Three-day cycle of learning plan with reflection Unit plans Design and use a classroom management plan Daily reflection log Design and execute a bulletin board Reflect on differentiation in your classroom Revise philosophy statement

Other

Figure 4-2   Grid for Charting Collected Evidence

INTASC Principles NAEYC Initial Licensure Standards	Evidence I already have	Evidence I still need

1.Knowledge of subject matter
    4b. Using developmentally effective approaches
    4c. Understanding content knowledge in early education
    4d. Building meaningful curriculum		

2. Knowledge of human development
    1. Promoting child development and learning
    4b. Using developmentally effective approaches
    4d. Building meaningful curriculum		

3. Instruction adapted for diverse learners
    1. Promoting child development and learning
    2. Building family and community relationships
    4b. Using developmentally effective approaches		

Figure 4-2   Grid for Charting Collected Evidence, continued

INTASC Principles NAEYC Initial Licensure Standards	Evidence I already have	Evidence I still need

4. Use of multiple strategies and resources
    4b. Using developmentally effective approaches
    4d. Building meaningful curriculum		

5. Learning environment/motivation and behavior
    1. Promoting child development and learning
    2. Observing, documenting, and assessing to
        support young children
        and families
    4b. Using developmentally effective approaches
    4d. Building meaningful curriculum		

6. Effective communication
    4a. Connecting with children and families
    4b. Using developmentally effective approaches		

7. Planning for instruction
    1. Promoting child development and learning
    2. Building family and community relationships
    3. Observing, documenting, and assessing to
        support young children
        and families
    4a. Connecting with children and families
    4b. Using developmentally effective approaches
    4d. Building meaningful curriculum		

8. Assessment of student learning
    4. Observing, documenting, and assessing to
        support young children and families.		

9. Professional growth and reflection 5. Becoming a professional		

10. Interpersonal relationships
    2. Building family and community relationships
    4a. Connecting with children and families
    5. Becoming a professional		

Activity 4-1

Look at the lists of possible portfolio artifacts that correspond to INTASC Principles and NAEYC Standards (Table 3-2) or review the list of sample artifacts described by courses taught in many university early childhood programs (Figure 4-1). Using Figure 4-2, chart the collection of evidence that you have already collected and note the evidence that is still needed before completing the portfolio process.

Chapter 4 Identifying Artifacts

Summary

Artifacts are tangible evidence of your developing skills in the field of early childhood education. Choosing artifacts is a highly personal endeavor and depends on your stage of development. The artifacts you select should not be considered permanent. They should change over time, reflecting your continual growth as a professional.

Suggested Web Sites

California Arts Project answers questions on artifacts and evidence for portfolio entries.
http://csmp.ucop.edu/tcap/nbpts/faq/faq4.html

The Role of Critical Reflection in the Portfolio Process. On-line professional development from Johns Hopkins University and Morgan State University provides examples of artifacts.
http: www.sitesupport.org/module1/portfolio.htm

What is reflection? On-line from UW-Whitewater lists a number of appropriate artifacts.
www.uwstout.edu/careers/portfolios.shtml

References

Anatonek, J. L., McCormick, D. E., & Donato, R. (1997). The student teacher portfolio as autobiography: Developing a professional identity. *The Modern Language Journal, 81*, 5 -27.

Burke, K. (1999). *How to assess authentic learning (3rd ed.).* Arlington Heights, IL: Skylight Training.

Costantino, P. M., De Lorenzo, M. N., & Kobrinski, E. J.(2006). *Developing a Professional Teaching Portfolio: A Guide for Success (2nd ed.).* Boston: Allyn & Bacon.

Jones, M., & Shelton, M. (2006). *Developing your portfolio: Enhancing your learning and showing your stuff. A guide for the early childhood student or professional.* New York: Routledge.

.

CHAPTER 5

ELECTRONIC PORTFOLIOS

What are Electronic Portfolios?

Electric portfolios are "purposeful collection[s] of work, captured by electronic means, that serve as an exhibit of individual efforts, progress, and achievements in one or more areas" (Wiedmer, 1998). Digital portfolios may be presented on a computer, a disk, a CD-ROM, or may be sent as email attachments. They are created and delivered using software programs such as PowerPoint or on the web. Digital portfolios are also known as Web portfolios, Multimedia portfolios, E-portfolios, and Web folios (http://webportfolio.info/), although Web-based portfolios allow viewers to access information on-line at their leisure (Rieman & Okrasinski, 2007).

Recent technological advances have encouraged initiatives for electronic portfolios rather than print portfolios to document performance and learning (Cambridge, Kahn, Tompkins, & Yancey, 2001; Milman, 1999). Furthermore, many teacher preparation programs are turning to electronic portfolio systems to meet National Council of Accreditation of Teacher Education (NCATE) requirements (Barrett & Knezek, 2003; Young, 2002).

Technology is the way of the future! The advancing use and influence of technology in higher education have caused some institutions to consider or require electronic portfolios. Some research shows that pre-service teachers who capture information in the form of text, graphics, audio, and video produce a multimedia portrayal of their skills and accomplishments (Pollard, 2006) and are more apt to incorporate technology into their own classrooms (Barrett, 2000; Wallace & Porter, 2004). Most importantly, creating an electronic portfolio allows you to demonstrate your technical skill, show your knowledge of current hard and software, and document your ability to meet technology standards (Wiedmer, 1998; Rieman & Okrasinski, 2007). The National Educational Technology Standards for Teachers (NETS*T) developed six standards areas with performance indicators to comply with most state, university, and district guidelines. Some states also have developed their own technology standards. To find your state's technology standards, begin by searching your State Department of Education web site.

Unlike traditional paper portfolios, electronic portfolios can be made interactive with the use of PowerPoint, Hyperlinks, sound, and video. "An electronic portfolio can be more flexible and dynamic than paper because multimedia provides an adaptable structure to present artifacts that convey the vitality of our profession" (Heath, 2002).

What are Web-Based Portfolios?

Web-based portfolios, sometimes known as webfolios, are designed to be published and viewed on the web. You create a web page on which to display your portfolio, and that web page is posted to a server. Software such as Microsoft FrontPage, LiveText, or TaskStream can be used to design web pages. The video feature of the web-based portfolios provides for in-depth self-assessment. For example, teaching episodes can be used as tools for peer evaluation and feedback from supervisors and mentors, thus providing you with strong insights of your professional growth.

Because web-based portfolios are stored on university servers rather than on your own computer, two problems could occur. There might be costs associated with site license fees and renting storage space on the server and/or you might be limited by the space available to you on a web server. Furthermore, this type of portfolio demands a higher level of technical skill. The time needed to acquire web-authoring skills can be challenging. Web-based electronic portfolios can be accessed any time by anyone with on-line capacity, and are therefore, less secure. Protecting your web site with a password may ensure confidentiality, but it is recommended that personal data, photographs of children, letters of recommendation, or other similar documents be copyrighted. Even then, your work could be copied and used by others.

What are Non-Web-Based Portfolios?

An alternative to building an electronic portfolio as a web page is developing a Microsoft Word presentation. This can be saved to a DVD or flash drive, you can create your own CD-ROM, or the document can be converted to a web page. Helpful resources for using Microsoft Word include Office 97 help tutorials and MS Word 2000 tutorial. Non web-based portfolios are created using presentation software such as PowerPoint, a software application within Microsoft Office that includes a word processing program (Microsoft Word) and a spreadsheet application program (Excel). This program is easy to learn and use, allows for creativity and flexibility, and includes a range of tools to individualize documents. Electronic files can be easily saved to a CD-ROM, which increases your capacity to include text, graphics, audio, and/or video clips. This type of portfolio is secure; material is easy to store, and the portfolio is simple to duplicate and distribute. The popularity of the software makes viewing uncomplicated.

Hardware Needed to Create Electronic Portfolios

You need a computer with sufficient memory for storage (20-80 GB), sufficient memory for processing (128 MB to 1 GB of RAM), video input and output ports, and any or all of the following drives: flash drives, CD-RW or DV-RW (Costantino et al., 2006; Pastore, 2005). In addition, you need a printer, a flat-bed color scanner, a microphone, a digital still camera or digital video camera if you plan to incorporate video clips, a CD burner if you choose to publish your portfolio on a CD, a DVD burner if you want to publish your portfolio on a DVD, and a flash drive or other external drive for backup or transfer of digital assets. You can store your electronic portfolio on a flash drive, a CD, a DVD, or on the web as an html, pdf, or as a Word file, PowerPoint or HyperStudio document. Microsoft Word and PowerPoint files can be sent directly to the web; however, if you plan to publish your portfolio on the Internet, you will need Internet service access. Any program that can create multimedia and/or web pages can be appropriate for electronic portfolios.

Organizing Your Electronic Portfolio

Just as with a paper portfolio, the process of gathering and keeping track of information over time necessitates an organized approach to documentation and storage. It is very helpful in the design phase to create a flowchart as a visual representation of the content of your portfolio and the manner in which your artifacts are linked to the standards. Once your artifacts have been selected, and you have mapped out how they will connect to the standards, you can begin the actual development process. During this phase you will incorporate all your artifacts, whether they are text, digital photographs, audio, or video into a completed program stored on either a CD-ROM, DVD, or flash drive (Campbell et al., 2007).

The collection and archiving of work can be facilitated by using a number of computer-based programs ranging from spreadsheet applications for the organization of student data such as Grade Quick by Jackson Software to multimedia presentation software with portfolio applications like Hyperstudio's Portfolio Assessment Toolkit by Knowledge Adventure, Electronic Portfolio by Scholastic, and web-based programs such as TaskStream. All of these programs have the potential to greatly impact the ways in which authentic assessment is used (Barrett, 2001; Murphy & Richards, 2005).

Benefits of Electronic Portfolios

Electronic portfolios, like paper portfolios, are used by pre-service teachers to demonstrate their skills and competencies as they enter the professional field. Advantages to electronic portfolios are that they are compact, easy to store and distribute, and inexpensive to duplicate. They can be viewed anywhere with appropriate equipment. The hyperlink feature common to E-portfolios facilitates an easily modifiable and more flexible structure than is possible in print versions, and allows easy and efficient navigation through the documents. The ability to include more types of information is paramount. Videotapes of one's teaching performance, audiotapes of children reading, pictures of three-dimensional sculptures or constructions, scanned artifacts of student work, as well as text entries, allow you to display your technical competence of computer knowledge and familiarity with software applications. This is now a desirable quality for today's teachers. In addition, creativity, active learning, enhanced self-confidence, and dissemination to a broader community are other major advantages of electronic portfolios (Kilbane & Milman, 2003).

Evaluating Electronic Portfolios

Electronic portfolios can be evaluated like traditional paper portfolios, although often additional scoring criteria are added to address the technical aspects of this type of portfolio. Figure 5-1 provides an example of an electronic portfolio rubric, where specific requirements are listed in the leftmost column and point values ranging from 1 to 5 and criteria appear across the top. (Martin, 1999). This rubric could be adjusted to meet the requirements of a particular course, instructor, or institution.

Figure 5-1   Sample Scoring Rubric for Electronic Portfolios

Standard Being Evaluated	Unsatisfactory 1 Point Detracts from overall presentation	Basic 2 points Neither adds nor detracts	Proficient 3 points Helps communicate message	Distinguished 4 points Enhances presented information
Title Page				
Introduction				
Organization				
Navigability				
Audio/Video Selections				

(Adapted from Martin, 1999)

Activity 5-1

Select a web site featuring electronic portfolios. Or explore a web-based portfolio creation solution with a 30-day free trial and try it out. Come up with your own conclusion about whether or not the electronic portfolio is for you. For example, you might go to the Inspiration Web site and download a free 30-day trial version of Inspiration 6, if you don't already have a copy. Take a look at James Rye's example of a basic portfolio document using Inspiration. Then, design your portfolio layout in Inspiration. Save your file as "Portfolio Design." Be specific about the categories, components, and artifacts you intent to include in your portfolio. Post your Inspiration file as an attachment on PLACES Portfolio Lesson 2 Just For Fun Folder, along with a paragraph of questions, comments, or concerns you may have about the portfolio. Reply to one other person's posting giving helpful suggestions or comments. (http:///www.schools.pinellas.k12.fl.us/itu/classfavie/Lesson5.2.html).

Summary

Basically, creating an electronic portfolio involves the processes of both portfolio development and multimedia development. Electronic portfolios require technical skill and access to technical support, which print versions do not. Still there are many advantages to electronic portfolios. They are easy to store and inexpensive to reproduce and distribute. They can be viewed anywhere with appropriate equipment. They are more flexible in structure than print versions, and allow for easy and efficient navigation through the documents. Furthermore, the ability to include graphics, audio and/or video clips, as well as text, allows for interactive, innovative, and dynamic presentations.

However, both paper and electronic portfolios involve collecting materials, selecting materials, and reflecting on the materials. They merely differ in how they are produced. The stages for developing an electronic portfolio will be discussed more fully in Chapters 7, 8, and 9 along with the steps for developing a paper portfolio.

Suggested Web Sites

Barrett, Helen, the Educational Technology Coordinator for the School of Education, University of Alaska Anchorage, has a rich collection of web resources on alternative assessment and electronic portfolios at http://www.helenbarrett.com/Portfolios/bookmarks.html.

Burns, J. *An introduction to HTML.* http://www.htmlgoodies.com/primers/primer_1.html

Elder, I. has published advice to potential electronic portfolio developers at http:/www.mwsc.edu/~edexp/studentview2.html.

Examples of video for peer-to-peer tool evaluations can be viewed at http:www.towson.edu/~kirmani/teachertraining/.

HyperStudio is a multimedia authoring program that can be saved to your own CD-ROM. The HyperStudio tutorial from Learning Space and Self-Paced HyperStudio workshop are additional references located at http://www.HyperStudio.com.

K-12 Electronic Portfolios are available at this site. https://webfolios.home.netcome.com

Links to a variety of teaching portfolios on-line are available at these sites: http://www.utep.edu. and http://www.unf.edu/. Then, type in the word *portfolios.*

McGraw-Hill Companies: http://www.folioLive.com is an electronic portfolio tool.

National Educational Technology Standards for Students (NETS*T) developed six standard areas with performance indicators to comply with most state, university, and district guidelines. http://www.iste.org/ or http://cnets.iste.org/

Ryan, P. (2003). In *Essential elements of electronic portfolio* the author explains ethical and copyright guidelines and provides background resources for the Internet. http:www.towson.edu/~pryan/eportfolio or www.towson.edu/~pryan/eportfolio/resources.htm

State technology standards for the State of Maryland are available at www.mcps.k12.md.us/departments/technologya/techstandards/checklist

References

Barrett, H. C. (2000). Create your own electronic portfolio: Using off-the-shelf software to showcase your own or student work. *Learning and Leading with Technology, 27* (7), 14-21.

Barrett, H. C. (2001). Electronic portfolios. In A. Kovalchick and K. Dawson (Eds.), *Education and technology: An encyclopedia.* Santa Barbara, CA: ABC-CLIO.

Barrett, H. C., & Knezek, D. (2003). *E-Portfolios: Issues in assessment, accountability and pre-service teacher preparation.* Paper presented at the Annual Meeting of the American Educational Research Association, Chicago, IL, 2003.

Burns, J. *An introduction to HTML.*[On-line] http://www.htmlgoodies.com/primers/primer_1.html Retrieved January 15, 2007.

Cambridge, B., Kahn, S., Tompkins, D., & Yancey, K. (Eds.) (2001). *Electronic portfolios: Emerging practices in student, faculty, and institutional learning,* Washington, DC: American Association for Higher Education.

Campbell, D. M., Cignetti, P. B., Melenyzer, B. J., Nettles, D. H., & Wyman, R. M. (2007). *How to develop a professional portfolio: A manual for teachers* (4th ed.). Boston: Allyn & Bacon.

Costantino, P. M., De Lorenzo, M. N., & Kobrinski, E. J. (2006). *Developing a professional teaching portfolio: A guide for success* (2nd ed.). Boston: Allyn & Bacon.

Heath, M. (2002). Electronic portfolios for reflective self-assessment. *Teacher Librarian, 30* (1), 19-23.

Jackson Software. GradeQuick [Software package]. Glencoe, IL: Author.

Kilbane, C., & Milman, N. (2003). *The digital teaching portfolio handbook: A how-to-guide for educators.* Boston: Allyn & Bacon.

Knowledge Adventure: Hyperstudio [software package]. El Cajon, CA: Roger Wagner
    Publishing.

Martin, D. B. (1999). *The portfolio planner: Making professional portfolios work for you.*
    Upper Saddle River, NJ: Prentice Hall.

Maryland's Teacher Technology Standards. [On-line]
    http://www.mcps.k12.md.us/departments/technology/techstandards/checklist/   Retrieved   January   21,
    2007.

Microsoft Corporation. PowerPoint [Software package]. Redmond, WA: Author.

Milman, N. (1999). Web-based electronic teaching portfolios for preservice teachers. In J.
    Price et al. (Eds.), *Proceedings of the Society for Information Technology and Teacher
    Education International Conference 1999* (pp.1174-1179). Chesapeake, VA; AACE.

Murphy, K. L., & Richard, J. (2005). The promise of E-portfolios: Ownership and authentic
    assessment. *Integrated Technologies, Innovative Learning: Insights from the PT3
    Program.* International Society for Technology in Education.

National Educational Technology Standards for Teachers [On-line]
    http://cnets.iste.org/teachers/t_stands/html. Retrieved January 12, 2007.

Pastore, R. S. (2005). Webportfolio.info @ Teacherworldcom. [On-line] http://webportfolio.info/
    Retrieved November 2, 2006.

Pinellas School District. (2001). *Digital portfolios.* [On-line]
    http://www.schools.pinellas.k12.fl.us/itu/classfavie/Lesson5.2.html. Retrieved May 23, 2007.

Pollard, R. R. (2006). Showcasing new teachers: Electronic portfolios. [On-line]
    www.icte.org/T01_Library/T01_140.PDF. Retrieved January 17, 2007.

Rieman, P. L., & Okrasinski, J. (2007). *Creating your teaching portfolio* (2nd ed.). New York: McGraw-Hill.

Wallace, R.C., & Porter, R. (2004). *A call to arms for school learners: Can you assist students(s) market
    their skill(s) and competencies through electronic portfolios?* Society for Information Technology for
    Teachers in Education. SITE Conference, 2004; Atlanta, GA.

Webportfolio.info (2005). [On-line] http://webportfolio.info/ Retrieved November 2, 2006.

Wiedmer, T. L. (1998). Digital portfolios: Capturing and demonstrating skills and levels of
    performance. *Phi Delta Kappan, 79* (8), 586-589.

Young, J. (2002). E-Portfolios could give students a new sense of their accomplishments.
    Chronicle of Higher Education, 48 (26), 31-32.

CHAPTER 6

DEVELOPING A PHILOSOPHY OF EDUCATION STATEMENT

A philosophy of education can be defined as "the study of the purpose, process, and nature and ideals of education" (http://wikipedia.org). Another definition can be found in *Webster's Dictionary* as the science dealing with the general causes and principles of thing. Personal attitudes toward teaching send a clear message as to what your priorities and values are. As a pre-service intern beginning the exciting process of working with young children and their families, it's important to reflect on your beliefs and attitudes as they pertain to young children and your role as their teacher. Look at your philosophy of education as a work in process, growing and changing as you grow and change as a pre-service early childhood educator. In this chapter, we will identify *why* a philosophy of education is important, *where* it should be placed in your portfolio, and finally suggest *how* to go about writing your philosophy of education statement.

Why?

When asking pre-service interns why they want to enter the teaching profession, the answers are deeply personal and varied. Many students express how much they love children, how they have played teacher to their unsuspecting siblings and have always known that this field of work is their passion. Other interns share stories of teachers they had in elementary school, both good and bad. As we probe deeper and ask interns to elaborate as to what specifically is it that you like about working with young children, their individual attitudes, beliefs, and ideals begin to emerge. It is important to examine your personal beliefs to help frame how you want to interact with young children and their families. It will help you become a better teacher, with a clear direction of where you're going and how you want to get there.

It is recommended that you begin a philosophy of education statement early in your pre-service training, and make changes as your work and experience with young children strengthens. Even in your first early childhood course, you should try to develop a philosophy of education statement. Take the time to reflect on why you are entering the field of early childhood education and what personal attitudes and beliefs you hold. Examine your knowledge, background, prior and present experiences, observations, and discussions with early childhood professionals to assist you in determining what you hold to be important and the impact this will have on the lives of young children. As you take additional courses and engage in more fieldwork, you will grow as a professional. You will be exposed to early childhood from a historic perspective, and learn that the education of preschool-aged children "has proven to be an extremely important component of the total educational system" (Roopnarine & Johnson, 1987, p. 12). New ideas, theories of child development, and principles you will be learning about in your course work build a helpful framework to guide and strengthen your philosophy of education.

Your philosophy of education continues to evolve as you learn more and more about child development and learning theories. In ideal philosophy statements, logical connections are drawn between philosophical and theoretical foundations. Therefore, sources of theoretical support may assist you in addressing your ideas of how young children learn. Reflecting on the major theories of early childhood education is an effective method to help you begin a personal philosophy of education statement. Reviewing the summary of major learning theories that are summarized in Table 6-1 may help you identify the components that best exemplify your attitudes and beliefs.

Table 6-1   Summary of Early Childhood Learning Theories

Learning Theory	Basic Tenets of the Theory	Major Theorists
Basic Needs Theory	The hierarchy of humans' basic needs is often depicted as a pyramid consisting of five levels; higher needs can only be met if the lower ones are satisfied. Needs include physiological, safety, love, esteem, cognitive, aesthetic, self-actualization, and self-transcendence.	Maslow (1908-1970)
Behaviorism and Social Learning Theory	Behaviorism uses stimuli and responses, classical and operant conditioning, to develop behavior. Social learning theory emphasizes the role of modeling in developing behavior.	Skinner (1904-1990) Pavlov (1849-1936) Bandura (1977) Watson (1878-1958)
Cognitive-Developmental Theory	A theory that views children as actively constructing knowledge as they manipulate and explore their world; cognitive development takes place in stages.	Piaget (1896-1980)
Dynamic Systems Perspective	Common human genetics is dynamic, branching out in many directions. Each strand represents a potential area of skills within the major domains or child development—physical, cognitive, and social/emotional.	Fischer & Bidell (1998)
Ecological Systems Theory	Child's heredity joins with multiple levels of the surrounding environment from micro-systems to macro-systems to form development, patterns, relationships, personalities, and capacities.	Bronfenbrenner (1979; 1989; 1993)
Ethological Theory of Attachment	A theory that views infant-caregiver bonding as necessary for feelings of security and the capacity to form trusting relationships.	Bowlby (1980)
Information Processing Theory	An approach that views human mind as a symbol-manipulating system through which information flows; cognitive development is a continuous process.	Atkinson & Shiffrin (1968) Klahr & MacWhinney (1998)

Table 6-1   Summary of Early Childhood Learning Theories, continued

Learning Theory	Basic Tenets of the Theory	Major Theorists
Maturation Theory	Based on evolutionary ideas, child development was seen as a genetically determined series of events that unfold automatically.	Hall (1904); Gesell (1933)
Moral Development	Kohlberg's 6 stages explain the development of moral reasoning; they emerge from children's own thinking about moral problems, and are the basis for ethical behavior. Gilligan, critical of Kohlberg, based her theory on interrelationships of ethics, care, and compassion.	Kohlberg (1958a; 1975) Gilligan (1982)
Montessori's Educational Philosophy	Children learn on their own, and quite differently from adults. Her theory includes five sensitive periods: for order, for details, for the use of hands, for walking, and for language, and puts faith in Nature's laws guiding the child through child-centered education.	Montessori (1870-1952)
Multiple Intelligence Theory	This theory proposes at least eight independent intelligences based on distinct sets of processing operations that allow individuals to engage in a wide range of culturally valued activities.	Gardner (1983; 1993; 1998b)
Psychosocial Theory	Expands on Freud's theory, emphasizing psychosocial outcomes at each of 8 stages of development; personality, attitudes, and skill development help children become active members of their society.	Erikson (1902-1994)
Socio-cultural theory	Children acquire ways of thinking and behaving that come from a community's culture and from cooperative experiences with adults or more experienced peers.	Vygotsky (1896-1934)

(Berk, 2006; Crain, 2000; Puckett & Black, 2005)

A clearly written philosophy statement not only helps you as a reflective practitioner in the field of early childhood education; it can assist in the employment process. Upon graduation, a philosophy statement of education is an important document that identifies your belief as a novice teacher. In a competitive market place, your philosophy of education statement will help set you apart from the competition and provide school personnel with a clear understanding of who you are as an educator. Moreover, it can be of value in the promotion and tenure process. Since this statement covers numerous issues, it must be very concise. Usually philosophy statements are one page in length. While the writing can vary, a straightforward narrative approach is recommended. The best way to articulate your passion for teaching and children is through a meaningful, genuine, and clearly written philosophy of education statement.

Where?

The philosophy of education statement is the first document of the portfolio. It is the first item read by portfolio assessors and potential employers. The philosophy of education statement is the starting point, and it creates an initial and lasting impression. It should be concise, clearly written, and true to whom you are as an early childhood educator. You will be judged on your written expression, sentence structure, and ability to communicate your thoughts, attitudes, and beliefs about teaching. As you write, keep in mind your audience and abstain from controversial or political comments that may offend the reader. For example, if you feel that all mothers should stay at home to raise young children, and you are presenting your portfolio to a working mother, this attitude could possibly generate an unnecessary bias against you. This may sound obvious, but it has been done before!

How?

How can I develop a philosophy of education statement when my experience working with young children is limited? This is a question frequently asked by pre-service interns early in their careers. For many of you, your experience working with young children is limited to babysitting, working in child care, or assisting in a classroom. You do, however, have many years as a student, and you know what you like and dislike about your classroom experiences as a learner. The following questions can help get you started:

> * Why do I want to become an early childhood educator?
> * How do I define a teacher?
> * What method of teaching is most effective?
> * What knowledge do I need to be effective working with young children?
> * What is my view of the role of the family and community?
> * What theories or philosophies support my ideas?
> * How do I wish to be remembered by my students? (http://resumes-for-teachers).
> * Why is teaching an important career?
> * What are the obstacles facing children and families and how can I help them to overcome these obstacles? (http://resumes-for-teachers).

Spend time thinking about these questions and record some ideas. Your philosophy of education statement will begin to emerge as you reflect on your experiences as a teacher and learner.

Strategies to Get You Started

An effective starting point for a pre-service teacher is to find a meaningful quote that exemplifies his or her beliefs about teaching and young children. From there, go on to explain in the body of your philosophy answers to the questions above. Spend time researching quotes and determine if there is one of particular personal meaning to you. Some may find it easier to express their beliefs in the form of a poem, while others may use a bullet format where their beliefs are expressed in concise and brief statements. Your college or university department of education should have a conceptual framework or philosophy guiding course work and experiences. Reading and understanding this document may give you ideas for your personal philosophy statement. Take the time, be reflective, and you'll be surprisingly pleased with the results!

Philosophy of Education and Reflective Practice

As stated earlier, a philosophy of education statement is a work in progress—growing and changing as you gain experience, increased commitment, and understanding of the field of early childhood education. Make sure you continue to reflect upon your statement throughout your years as a pre-service teacher. The philosophy of education statement you write as a freshman in college will most likely not be the same document you use during your final portfolio presentation or during a job interview. You may find that your beliefs change as you work in the field, and your philosophy should change as well. Continue to reflect on your experiences and make the necessary changes so that your statement is personal, honest, meaningful, and one that accurately describes you as an early childhood practitioner.

It is always helpful to see models of what professors deem exemplary work. Two samples (Figures 6-1 and 6-2) are exemplary examples of philosophy statements written by freshman or college students in their early stages of developing a philosophy of education. Figures 6-3 and 6-4 are models of philosophy statements from Showcase Portfolios. You will notice that each philosophy statement expresses the views of a particular individual.

Figure 6-1   Early Philosophy Statement

PHILOSOPHY OF EDUCATION

I believe that . . .

Each child is a gift.

Fun equates to engaging in active learning.

My job has great significance.

Each child is significant and has special needs.

A teacher is a facilitator of education.

Teaching will not only benefit the children, but also myself.

Children learn by interaction and play.

Communication between facilitator and parents is very important.

I can touch and impact children's lives.

I will be a great teacher because it is such a huge part of who I am

And who I want to be.

Figure 6-2   Early Philosophy Statement

My Philosophy of Education Statement

I believe

that the goal of education is assisting children in discovering the different aspects of life. I believe it is important to give all children the opportunity and time to develop their minds at their own pace, but at the same time challenge them to think on their own rather than just listening to the educators' own knowledge.

I believe

that knowledge is gained through experiences. A child needs more than just someone standing in front of them telling them what is right and wrong. Children need to see and experience different concepts to let them come to an understanding on their own. Knowledge cannot be forced on them, but directed to what amuses their minds.

I believe

that the role of a teacher is to know each of her students and the way that learning comes naturally for them. A teacher should offer different aspects of teaching allowing students to understand fully. Educators should allow children to feel comfortable and have complete trust in showing and sharing their weaknesses and problems. A teacher should not only be there for educational support, but also for emotional support. A teacher should let children know that if there are any problems, whether in or outside of the classroom, that the teacher is always there for guidance.

I believe

that all children should have the opportunity to a full education. Children are born learners and are seeking someone to show them the world. In fact, children are our future. Also, children are not only learning from the teacher, but at the same time, the teacher is learning from her own students. All children should know that one is never too big to ask questions and one never knows too much to learn something new.

I believe

that a teacher should build and keep strong working relationships with parents and colleagues. A teacher should allow parents to know and be involved in what is going one in and outside of the classroom. Teacher and parents should have a strong communication relationship in regards to their children's education and health. A teacher should reflect with colleagues to share ideas and experiences within the classroom, so that all can learn from each other.

Figure 6-3   Showcase Portfolio Philosophy Statement

My Personal Philosophy of Education

Defining my personal philosophy of education is truly a daunting task. There are so many things I've learned and so much I want to incorporate that I could easily fill an entire book. Therefore, in order to keep this brief, I have selected a few quotes that I find reflect at least some of what I believe is important in the education of young children.

> "Students learn what they care about . . . "Stanford Ericksen has said, but Goethe knew something else: "In all things we learn only from those we love." Add to that Emerson's declaration: "The secret of education lies in respecting the pupil," and we have a formula something like this: "Students learn what they care about, from people they care about and who, they know, care about them . . . "
> -Barbara Harrell Carson, 1996, *Thirty Years of Stories.*

It is vital that children feel loved, accepted, valued, and respected. Young children are open-hearted; they will respond to those who love them. It is also important for children to feel that what they are learning and doing in the classroom is valuable and interesting, not just beneficial.

> "Tell me and I forget. Show me and I remember. Involve me and I understand." -
> Chinese proverb

> "A mind is a fire to be kindled, not a vessel to be filled."   -Plutarch

> "If children are excited, curious, resourceful, and confident about their ability to figure things out and eager to exchange opinions with other adults and children, they are bound to go on learning, particularly when they are out of the classroom and throughout the rest of their lives.   -Constance Kamii

I see my role in the educational process as pivotal. It is up to every teacher to kindle the love of learning, the excitement, curiosity, and confidence in all of the children entrusted to his or her care. In all activities, the teacher serves as a model who can foster lifelong learning, respect, self-awareness, self-esteem, patience, and kindness. We can nurture all manner of high ideas, or not.

Figure 6-4   Showcase Portfolio Philosophy Statement

<u>Philosophy of Education Statement</u>

"Too often we give out children answers to remember rather than problems to solve."
-Roger Lewin

This quote describes a large part of my educational philosophy, because it emphasizes that process is more important than content in the education of children. Content is the information that children learn, such as math facts, letters, words. Process is the ability to be able to problem solve and think critically. It is the process by which children come to an answer that is more important than the answer itself. Children need to learn how to problem solve and think critically much more than they need to memorize facts. Children who learn how to tackle a problem and think critically about a situation will be able to use these skills for their entire lives. Later in life, children will be presented with many problems to solve, whether in their careers or their daily lives. Children might benefit from memorizing their multiplication facts, and this memorization will indeed come in useful later in life, but the more critical thing is to teach children how to work out multiplication problems for themselves. If children are taught why two times two equals four through the use of manipulative blocks and hands-on materials, they will understand multiplication.   However, if children are taught to memorize two times two without understanding why this is, they will not understand multiplication and will not be able to solve new problems when they arise.

"Intelligence plus character—that is the goal of true education."
-Martin Luther King, Jr.

This is another quote that is a major part of my philosophy of education. I believe that it is essential for children to learn about good character as well as to learn academics. I know that in many schools character education is a major part of the curriculum. Children are taught respect, caring, trustworthiness, responsibility, fairness, and citizenship. I believe that learning these pillars of good character is important. Children who can learn to be responsible will learn to turn assignments in on time and take responsibility for their own futures. Children who are taught respect will learn to have good relations with other people. Children who are taught to be trustworthy will be relied upon and trusted. Having a good character is an essential part of being successful in a future career. Employers and college professors need to know that they can rely on their students and employees. I plan to incorporate character education in my future classrooms in many ways. I will make sure the six pillars of good character are on the wall, so that my students can be reminded of them throughout the day. I will also praise and recognize students who show good character in their lives.

Activity 6-1

Hopefully, reading the four philosophy statements will get your creative juices flowing! Begin by writing three words that describe you as a teacher.

1. _____
2. _____
3. _____

Write three beliefs you have about teaching.

1. _____
2. _____
3. _____

Identify three attributes of a good teacher.

1. _____
2. _____
3. _____

Now, using these guides, try writing a philosophy statement that sums up your beliefs about children, families, teaching, and learning. How do you view yourself as an early childhood professional?

Summary

Understanding that your philosophy statement is a work in progress is a key idea, and we recommend that you update your philosophy statement annually. By examining your personal beliefs, your ideas about schools and schooling, your understandings about people that are like you and different from you, you tell the readers what you want them to know about you. Furthermore, writing your statement provides an opportunity for personal growth and satisfaction. It is critical that the writing be reflective, personal, and clear, and that your final document be well-organized and error-free, giving reviewers a vivid picture of you as a professional early childhood educator.

Suggested Web Sites

If you need additional ideas, the Internet is full of examples of various types of philosophy statements. We found samples that were written in various styles at the following sites.

oregonstate.edu/instruct/ed416/sample.html
www.schoolmarm.org/portfolio/gen-phil.htm
reach.ucf.edu/~ed_found/gpi.html

References

Berk, L. E. (2006). *Child development* (7th ed.). Boston: Allyn & Bacon.

Crain, W. (2000). *Theories of development: Concepts and application* (4th ed.). Upper Saddle
  River, NJ: Prentice Hall.

Puckett, M. B., & Black, J. K. (2005). *The young child: Development from prebirth through age
  eight* (4th ed.). Upper Saddle River, NJ: Merrill/Prentice Hall.

Roopnarine, J. L., & Johnson, J. E. (2005). *Approaches to early childhood education* (4th ed.). Upper Saddle
  River, NJ: Merrill/Prentice Hall.

CHAPTER 7

WRITING YOUR REFLECTIVE NARRATIVE

What is Reflection?

Reflection, the act of being contemplative, thoughtful, or meditative, is the defining characteristic of the portfolio. Through reflection, you show your thinking about children, content, development, diversity, motivation, classroom management, technology, collaboration, planning, implementing, and assessing lessons based on substantive standards. Reflection shows where your practice and pedagogy merge. The process of reflecting enhances self-evaluation of your teaching and learning, bringing together fresh experiences and prior information to form new knowledge.

What is a Reflective Narrative?

A reflective narrative is *not* a caption! A caption simply labels in one or two sentences what the artifact in your portfolio is. Captions are acceptable for items contained in the Appendix, such as letters from parents or students, or photographs not specific to a lesson or activity. Artifacts used as evidence of INTASC or NAEYC standards *must* be accompanied by a reflective narrative that explains why the evidence or document was chosen to be included in the portfolio and why it serves as evidence for one of the standards or principles.

How Your Reflective Narrative Relates to Your Philosophy Statement

Your personal learning experiences, teaching style, and philosophy define who you are as a young professional. Your ideas and understandings about teaching and learning are a product of your prior educational experiences, life occurrences, and the observations you have made about children's development in the classroom. As you learned in Chapter 6, your portfolio usually begins with your philosophy--a concise statement that combines educational theory and pedagogy with practice.

The artifacts in your portfolio, accompanied by reflective narrative should be an extension of your philosophy. Here you have the opportunity to select artifacts for inclusion in your portfolio that will infuse your personal beliefs and values by relating them to your understanding of theory and practice. Instructional lesson plans presented alone in a portfolio are just that, instructional lesson plans. An artifact without any explanation of learning has no meaning to the reader or reviewer. The reflective narrative that accompanies an artifact is what separates a portfolio from a scrapbook or simply a collection of materials. Reflection is what shows your learning, growth, and understanding over time. It is where beliefs and values meet educational theory in the quest to become a reflective practitioner.

What Does a Reflective Narrative Look Like?

A reflective narrative should have a purpose. It is not a mere caption. It is not a summary of a lesson. It should focus on the processes and products of your growth. This understanding is so important that it becomes a part of your everyday teaching. The reflective narrative is broken into several parts that combine knowledge and experience. These parts are listed below in Figure 7-1.

Figure 7-1   Parts of a Reflective Narrative

- What is the artifact?

- How does the artifact connect to the INTASC principles and NAEYC standards?

- How does this artifact contribute to my learning?

- In what way does this artifact contribute to my positive impact on student learning?

- Where does this artifact fit within the core cluster of instructional activities?
  (Judging prior learning and background knowledge, Planning instruction, Teaching, Assessing, Analyzing, and Reflecting)

How Does the Artifact Connect to the INTASC Principles and NAEYC Standards?

Connecting your artifact to the INTASC standards takes thought and practice. One helpful resource is the *Model Standards for Beginning Teacher Licensing, Assessment and Development* (1992) developed by Interstate New Teacher Assessment and Support Consortium. This document, available on-line at www.ccsso.org/content/pdfs/corestrd.pdf, addresses each principle by elaborating on the knowledge, dispositions, and performances required for each INTASC principle. If your school uses a rubric for assessment, the indictors for meeting the standard may also help you better understand each principle. Our university uses the same portfolio assessment form (see Table 7-1) throughout the portfolio development process, as well as for the final summative assessment. This document is divided into sections based on the INTASC Principles. The INTASC Principles are in Column 1; the indicators that fall under each standard are in Column 2. This document is helpful in understanding what reviewers are looking at and looking for. Using some of the language of the indicators in your reflective narrative helps adjudicators know that you have met the standard. For example, if you include a lesson plan under INTASC #1, you might describe the national, state, or local standards used in your plan (indicator 1). You might show how you linked content to students' prior learning (indicator 3). You might focus on key ideas of a particular curriculum (indicator 2).

Table 7-1   Portfolio Assessment Tool

INTASC Principles NAEYC Core Standards	Indicators

1. Knowledge of subject matter
   4b. Using developmentally effective approaches
   4c. Understanding content knowledge in early education
   4d. Building meaningful curriculum
	• Connections to the national/state/local standards of the discipline
	• Focused instruction on key ideas and methods of inquiry in the discipline
	• Content linked to students' prior understandings

2. Knowledge of human development
   1. Promoting child development and learning
   4b. Using developmentally effective approaches
   4d. Building meaning curriculum
	• Knowledge of typical and atypical growth and development
	•Instruction designed to meet learner's current need based on age, development, learning style, readiness, ability, culture, social group and/or values.

3. Instruction adapted for diverse learners
   1. Promoting child development and learning
   2. Building family and community relationships
   4b. Using developmentally effective approaches
	• Differentiated instruction for diverse and inclusive community of learners/students (e.g., diversity factors include but are not limited to race, ethnicity, religion, region, gender, language, socio-economic status, age, and individuals with exceptionalities or unique learning styles)
	• Evidence of multiple perspectives in subject matter

4. Use of multiple strategies and resources
   4b. Using developmentally effective approaches
   4d. Building meaningful curriculum
	• Variety of instructional strategies (including assessment) to achieve different purposes and meet students' needs
	• Instruction encouraging critical thinking/problem solving

5. Learning environment/motivation and behavior
   1. Promoting child development and learning
   3. Observing, documenting, and assessing to support young children and families
   4b. Using developmentally effective approaches
   4d. Building meaningful curriculum
	• Classroom management plan provides a positive, productive learning environment
	• Strategies to engage students in active learning
	• Encouragement of students' assuming responsibility for their own learning
	• Efficient use of instructional time
	• Collaboration with team members, administrators, and parents to promote positive behavior

Table 7-1   Portfolio Assessment Tool, continued

INTASC Principles NAEYC Core Standards	Indicators

6. Effective communication
   4a. Connecting with children and families
   4b. Using developmentally effective approaches
	• Demonstration of professional use of oral and written language skills
	• Integrated instructional application of appropriate technologies
	• Application of technology to meet professional needs.

7. Planning for instruction
   1. Promoting child development and learning
   2. Building family and community relationships
   3. Observing, documenting, and assessing to support young children and families
   4a. Connecting with children and families
   4b. Using developmentally effective approaches
   4d. Building meaningful curriculum
	• Creation of daily and long-term plans aligned with national/state/local curriculum goals, students' needs and prior knowledge and strategies for active learning
	• Use of assessment data to adjust instruction

8. Assessment of student learning 3. Observing, documenting, and assessing to support young children and families.	• Use of assessment plan to demonstrate positive impact on student learning • Use of pre- and post-assessments as well as formative assessment to diagnose, monitor, and document student progress • Use of information obtained from review of student work to plan and modify instruction
9. Professional growth and reflection 5. Becoming a professional	• Integration of classroom observation and analysis of data about students to evaluate the outcomes of teaching and to revise practice • Consultation of professional literature, colleagues, and other professional learning opportunities to advance student learning • Evidence of positive impact of professional development of student achievement

10. Interpersonal relationships
   2. Building family and community relationships
   4a. Connecting with children and families
   5. Becoming a professional
	• Participation in collegial activities, directed at the improvement of teaching and learning.
	• Effective communication with families, teachers, resource personnel to foster student learning and success
	• Identification and use of community resources to foster student learning and success

(Department of Early Childhood Education, Towson University)

Connecting your work to a specific standard is the first step that links theory to practice. For example, a lesson plan that teaches children how to use various word strategies to define two-tier vocabulary words in a story (Beck, McKeown, & Kucan, 2002) could demonstrate your learning within INTASC Principle #4: The teacher understands and uses and variety of instructional strategies to encourage students' development of critical thinking, problem solving, and performance skills. How you describe this relationship defines your learning and understanding of this INTASC Principle.

How does this same artifact represent your thinking and learning of the indicators in this standard? This lesson plan could represent the understanding of INTASC #4 because it shows that you can plan, implement, and assess a lesson using a variety of instructional strategies for a particular group of students. The reflective narrative explains your rationale for planning this lesson and illustrates how it was implemented. For example, "This artifact is included within INTASC Principle 4 as an example of using a variety of instructional strategies to encourage development. The artifact demonstrates specific word instruction and word learning strategies to promote repeated exposure to words."

The following is an excerpt from Kate's professional portfolio:
"In our reading class we learned about the importance of teaching vocabulary in context. Through working with students in small group settings and using pre-assessment data, I determined that many students in this second grade class did not know or use strategies to determine the meaning of unknown words. This assignment gave me the opportunity to see the impact and motivation of using context clues when teaching vocabulary. I also learned the importance of repeated exposure to the new vocabulary words. Students learned to ask questions, use the information in context, and use illustrations to help them define unknown words. Using the words in another sentence helped them to apply this knowledge outside of the text. Students used the strategies taught in this lesson during their independent reading time. This informal assessment provided me the opportunity to see the students use what they learned. I learned the importance of discussion when students are reading a new or unfamiliar text. Students were provided the opportunity to preview the text and write down words that were not familiar to them before they read. When we came to the unknown words, students were taught strategies for determining the meaning using context and picture clues."

Kate continues to explain what she already knew that was applied during her teaching, "I knew that each student learns in his or her own way. I also understood that motivation is a key factor when students are reading. I believe the students were more motivated to read this unfamiliar text after they previewed the book, made predictions, and wrote down unfamiliar words."

Here, Kate lets us know how her reflections of this lesson will improve or alter her teaching in the future. "Reviewing the assessment information from this lesson enabled me to plan accordingly for the next reading lesson, as well as to know whom to assist with this skill during independent reading. Teaching this lesson to a group of second grade students also highlighted the importance of students reading 'Just Right Texts' during independent reading time for all of us."

How does this reflection connect with Kate's philosophy of teaching? "To blend learning with fun is one of the values incorporated into my philosophy of teaching. I strive to do this in every lesson I plan. Students need to verbalize their thinking and learn to take risks. I believe this makes them better thinkers and learners. This lesson enabled children to discuss and confirm their thinking and take risks."

Parts of the Reflective Narrative

Each narrative should include the following components:

- A description of what the artifact is
- A rationale as to why the artifact was placed in the chosen INTASC/NAEYC principles and standards
- An explanation of how this artifact contributes to your professional growth as an early childhood educator
- A justification of how the artifact makes a positive impact on student learning
- A statement of where the artifact fits within the core cluster of instructional activities

---

Jenna describes her artifact by saying, "During my primary semester at Towson University, I was placed in a first grade classroom at RW Elementary School. While there, I planned and implemented a Mathematical Diagnostic Interview with one specific child in order to determine where that child's ability in mathematics lay." From this beginning, we know what this intern did, where she did it, why she did it, and the purpose of the activity.

A rationale is needed to explain why the artifact was placed in the chosen INTASC Principle and NAEYC Standard. Jenna's narrative continues, "I placed this plan under INTASC Principle #2 for many reasons. I designed this Interview to determine the student's current needs and abilities in relation to his age and development. I determined throughout this process that the child was learning above his developmental level. He was able to count aloud, distinguish between greater than and less than, identify numerals, and complete additional equations with given manipulatives. He also demonstrated the ability to do simple addition doubles facts mentally. I included this Interview under NAEYC Core Standard #3 because this whole assignment was based on the observation and documentation of an individual child. I used the information that I gathered throughout this assessment to determine the child's abilities and incorporate developmentally appropriate work on this his mathematical level."

Parts of the paragraph above also explain what Jenna had learned. She knew that the child possessed certain skills (counting, knowledge of greater and less than, identification of numerals, addition equations, mental math) that she could determine his developmental level to be above the norm. In Jenna's final sentence she explains how she used the information from the assessment to impact this child's learning.

Where does the artifact fit within the core cluster of instructional activities? In other words, is this artifact about judging prior learning, understanding background knowledge, planning instruction, teaching, assessing, analyzing, and/or reflecting? Is it about working collaboratively with other professionals, or using effective communication with families or school personnel? Does this artifact demonstrate using community resources to fostering success for all children? Did this artifact address issues of diversity including but not limited to race, ethnicity, religion, gender, language, socioeconomic status, age, exceptionalities, or learning styles? Does this artifact demonstrate use of technology as a classroom tool or as a way to advance professional goals? While a particular piece of evidence may "fit" into more than one area, you, the teacher candidate, select only one principle for it, and focus on how the evidence is representative of that standard.

Where would you place Jenna's artifact? While Jenna put this artifact under INTASC #2: The teacher understands how children learn and develop, someone else might place it under INTASC #8: The teacher understands and uses formal and informal assessment strategies to evaluate and ensure the continuous intellectual, social, and physical development of the learner.

Ten examples of high-caliber student narratives follow (see Figures 7-2 to 7-11). There is one example for each of the ten INTASC principles.

Figure 7-2

Course: SCIE 371: Teaching Science in ECED

Butterfly Life Cycle

INTASC Principle #1: The teacher understands the central concepts, tools of inquiry, and structures of the discipline(s) he or she teaches and creates learning experiences that make these aspects of subject matter meaningful for students.

NAEYC Standard 4c: Understand content knowledge in early education
Candidates understand the importance of each content area in young children's learning. They know the essential concepts, inquiry tools, and structure of content areas including academic subjects and can identify resources to deepen their understanding.

A 5E lesson plan is a constructivist method used primarily to teach mathematics or science in a primary classroom. It consists of five components: Engagement, Exploration, Explanation, Extension, and Evaluation. This artifact is a "5E" lesson plan, designed to teach students the life cycle of the butterfly and to help them remember the butterfly's life stages. The 5E format works very well when the intent is to help students explore science topics. I placed this science lesson plan under INTASC Principle 1, aligned with NAEYC Core Standard 4c, because I applied my understanding of the life science content area, scientific tools of inquiry, and my students' needs to the task of helping them remember the stages in order.

I combined the lesson with an art craft that helped them make connections between their prior knowledge and the facts that we read in the story in order to deepened their understanding. It also provided kinesthetic and tactile support. I added a song that also helped students recall the stages in order to support students with a musical intelligence. Throughout the lesson, my goal was to make the life cycle of the butterfly, which is an abstract concept, meaningful and concrete for my students.

While planning and teaching this lesson plan, I learned how important it is to help my students construct their own knowledge by building on what they already know. Critical thinking and making connections are important skills for all students.

Figure 7-3

Detective Dramatic Play Prop Box

Spring 2006~ECED341

INTASC Principle #2: The teacher understands how children learn and develop and can provide learning opportunities that support their intellectual, social, and personal development.

NAEYC Standard 4b: Using developmentally effective approaches
Candidates know, understand, and use a wide variety of effective approaches, strategies, and tools to positively influence young children's development and learning.

I designed a dramatic play prop box for my kindergarten class during my pre-primary placement. The use of the prop box in the classroom and the detective theme that I chose demonstrate my ability to create learning experiences that support all areas of young children's development. When children use the prop box for dramatic play, they enhance their social development through peer interactions and role-play. The props and literacy materials extend the children's understanding of the environment and support language skills. As children use their imaginations to become detectives, they break down sex and racial stereotypes and expectations, which enhances their personal development.

My knowledge of how young children learn tells me that children will solidify concepts through child-directed learning experiences and opportunities for social interaction. The detective theme lends itself well to these types of learning because children can investigate different items in the box and in the classroom and share their experiences with peers.

Prop boxes relate specifically to NAEYC's standard of developmentally appropriate practice. The detective theme bases itself on a child's intrinsic curiosity and helps to integrate all areas of the curriculum. I provided a variety of authentic, yet safe materials that enable the children to experience a rich classroom environment and participate in social interactions.

By completing this prop box, I learned that a teacher can be a facilitator of learning even when she is not executing direct instruction. The teacher must prepare the environment so that it is conducive to child exploration. Effective teachers can let go of their need to be in charge and recognize the value of dramatic play in promoting all areas of a child's development.

Figure 7-4

Course: Math 321.001 –Teaching Math in ECED

Math Lesson Plan

INTASC Principle #3: Learning styles/diversity
The teacher understands how students differ in their approaches to learning and creates instructional opportunities that are adapted to diverse learners.

NAEYC Standard 4c: Understand content knowledge in early education
Candidates understand the importance of each content area in young children's learning. They know the essential concepts, inquiry tools, and structure of content areas including academic subjects and can identify resources to deepen their understanding.

This artifact is the lesson plan I used to introduce the math concept of "one or two less than" to my first grade class at Glendale Elementary School. I feel that this lesson plan reflects INTASC #3 and NAEYC Standard 4c, because in planning it, I used my understanding of the different ways students learn and build knowledge. In my classes I learned that students vary their approaches to learning, and they use different types of intelligences in learning. Therefore, when planning this lesson, I included a variety of approaches in order to help my students use an intelligence that works well for them.

Also, in the "Teaching Math" class that I took the university, I learned the importance of having children explore their own ideas regarding ways to solve given mathematical problems. My understanding of this idea was further developed when I read an article examining a lesson that allowed the children to construct their own understanding of several math concepts. So, in addition to planning for diverse learners, I also included and encouraged opportunities for exploration.

Figure 7-5

Book Bag Comprehension Lesson

INTASC Principle #4: The teacher understands and uses a variety of instructional strategies to encourage students' development of critical thinking, problem solving, and performance skills.

NAEYC Standard 4d: Building meaningful curriculum
Candidates use their own knowledge and other resources to design, implement, and evaluate meaningful, challenging curriculum that promotes comprehensive developmental and learning outcomes for all young children.

For my Foundations of Language Arts course, I composed a book bag for the picture book <u>Scaredy Mouse</u> and wrote a lesson plan that incorporated the use of the book bag to enhance comprehension skills. The bag included props of the story characters. The bag itself was motivating because children did not know what was inside. The use of the book bag demonstrated my ability to use one of a wide variety of resources to enhance student learning. Because the highly motivating book bag engaged students in the lesson, I was able to achieve my comprehension objectives. Students used the book bag materials to be actively involved while I read the story. Following the reading, small groups of students used the book bag props to sequence the story events. My use of props for sequencing demonstrates my understanding of the cognitive processes associated with comprehension. Students are more likely to recall important information when they have a tactile and visual model of the event. My assessment for this book involved a unique flip book that I designed to match the text. By using a creative assessment tool rather than a standard pencil-and-paper worksheet, I was able to elicit children's strong performance skills.

This lesson aligns with NAEYC Standard 4d because I used high-quality resources to enhance students' thinking skills. My knowledge of the content area allowed me to plan a reading approach that engaged all students. I included many open-ended questions in my lesson plan so that I could assess students' thinking skills. This questioning during the reading demonstrated my ability to plan for students' responses and adjust my teaching based on them. By completing this book bag, I learned how teachers can promote higher-level thinking skills using unique instructional strategies and their own creativity.

Figure 7-6

Service-learning Project

INTASC Principle #5: Motivation and Classroom Management

NAEYC Standard 1: Promoting Child Development and Learning

This artifact is a service-learning project that I completed in my primary semester in a second grade classroom at Bear Creek Elementary School. It involved creating an interactive PowerPoint presentation on the mathematical concept of money. It also involved creating holiday math packets for the students to take home and work on over winter break. This allowed the students to refresh the skills that they learned throughout the semester. Also included is a report in which I documented the time spent on the project, the strategies used, and the benefits to children, their families, and the school community.

I chose to place this artifact under INTASC #5 because I collaborated with my mentor teacher, the children's parents, and other teachers at Bear Creek in order to complete this project. The children's parents were informed about the holiday math packets and the benefits of them. My mentor teacher needed to provide me with topics for both the PowerPoint presentation and the holiday math packets. The PowerPoint presentation was placed on the shared server at Bear Creek, so all teachers had access to it. The PowerPoint presentation was part of a classroom management plan in which differentiated instruction was essential. The more advanced students could work on this PowerPoint as an enrichment activity. Students were encouraged to assume responsibility for their own learning while completing the PowerPoint presentation and the math packets.

This artifact was also placed under NAEYC Standard 1 because I know that students learn best when topics and activities are interesting and engaging to them. The PowerPoint presentation was in the form of a story, and the students were able to click buttons to answer questions and make the story go on. The holiday math packets had an animal theme that the students found interesting and motivating. Using a PowerPoint presentation in the classroom created a challenging and supportive environment for students, where the learning they had been doing in math class was being reinforced.

While completing this service-learning project, I learned about the benefits of sending home holiday math packets. Students were able to refresh and reinforce important skills that they had learned, while spending time with their families. I learned that including interactive PowerPoint presentations in the classroom can be an excellent way to reinforce concepts, motivate learners, and challenge students who are more advanced.

Figure 7-7

Artifact: Collaborative Project Integrating Social Studies and Mathematics

INTASC Principle #6: The teacher uses knowledge of effective verbal, nonverbal and media communication techniques to foster active inquiry, collaboration, and supportive interaction in the classroom.

NAEYC Standard 5: Candidates identify and conduct themselves as members of the early childhood profession. They know and use ethical guidelines and other professional standards related to early childhood practice. They are continuous, collaborative learners who demonstrate knowledgeable, reflective, and critical perspectives on their work, making informed decisions that integrate knowledge from a variety of sources. They are informed advocates for sound educational practices and policies.

This was a collaborative project that I did with a peer in Math 321. There are several reasons that this artifact is under INTASC #6. The project presented how social studies and mathematics can be integrated. For the presentation, we created a PowerPoint of all our different ideas, using media communication as a way to foster active inquiry, collaboration, and support between our classmates, professor, and ourselves. The PowerPoint provided a visual for the learners that was supplemented by our presentation. Students were also given the opportunity to explore with hands-on materials independently before sharing ideas, using a nonverbal approach effectively. We also wrote a paper about what we learned during our research, thereby using a written approach to convey our learning effectively.

By working collaboratively with a partner and presenting to my classmates, I conducted myself as a professional member of the early childhood community. I communicated with my classmates, professor, and outside sources to create a meaningful presentation that promoted educational practices and policies for the classroom. For these reasons, this artifact is under NAEYC Standard 5. I learned that there are many ways to integrated social studies and mathematics.

Figure 7-8

Fluency Lesson

Course ECED 361 – Reading in Primary Grades

INTASC Principle #7: The teacher plans instruction based upon knowledge of subject matter, students, the community, and curriculum goals.

NAEYC Standard 4: Candidates integrate their understanding of and relationships with children and families; their understanding of developmentally effective approaches to teaching and learning, and their knowledge of academic disciplines, to design, implement, and evaluate experiences that promote positive development and learning for all children.

This artifact is the lesson plan and poem used for a fluency lesson in my first grade class at Glendale Elementary. I placed this artifact under INTASC 7 and aligned it with NAEYC Standard 4 because of all the things I needed to consider in designing this lesson.

First, the students were studying the Open Court reading topic "Things that Go," and extending knowledge about that topic is a curriculum goal. After this lesson, I knew the students would transition to writing things they know about bicycles. I wrote a poem about bicycles and included things they might know about bicycles in order to activate their prior knowledge. Exploring poetry was another goal, and I know the students enjoyed getting new poems for their poetry folders. Because I wanted to improve the students' expression in reading, I included prompts that would generate enthusiasm and excitement in the reading. I included sight words and decodable words to make the poem easy to read. Finally, I know that by reading the poem the children would enjoy making the sounds and saying the lines with gusto.

I integrated what I know of the students' likes and needs, the curriculum goals, the subject of fluency, and appropriate practice to create a lesson that would help all the students develop or improve their fluency in reading.

Figure 7-9

Artifact: Phonemic Awareness Assessment

INTASC Principle #8: The teacher understands and uses formal and informal assessment strategies to evaluate and ensure the continuous intellectual, social, and physical development of the learner.

NAEYC Standard 3: Candidates know about and understand the goals, benefits, and uses of assessment. They know about and use systematic observations, documentation, and other effective assessment strategies in a responsible way, in partnership with families and other professionals, to positively influence children's development and learning.

This artifact consists of several pieces. I gave a phonemic awareness screening to a student in first grade. Then, I analyzed his results and planned two activities for the areas when he needed assistance. From the results, I used the Continuum of Phonological Awareness to place the student and plan accordingly. Even though there were some areas that were higher scored than my stopping point, I had to use the guidelines that were provided for me. I stopped scoring when the student got 3/5 (or lower) correct. This artifact is under INTASC #8 because I used informal assessments to choose the child to screen; then I used formal assessments to evaluate him. From the formal assessments, I created activities that would ensure his intellectual growth as a learner. In return, the activities could also be done as a class, which would develop his social skills as well. Both activities used manipulatives, which also developed fine motor skills.

This artifact is under NAEYC Standard 3 because I used effective assessment strategies to create learning experiences that will positively influence his development and learning. This was the first time I had administered a formal assessment, which was a great learning experience.

Figure 7-10

Videotape Reflection

INTASC Principle #9: The teacher is a reflective practitioner who continually evaluates the effects of his/her choices and actions on others (students, parents, and other professionals in the learning community) and who actively seeks out opportunities to grow professionally.

NAEYC Standard 5: Candidates identify and conduct themselves as members of the early childhood profession. They know and use ethical guidelines and other professional standards related to early childhood practice. They are continuous, collaborative learners who demonstrate knowledgeable, reflective, and critical perspectives on their work, making informed decisions that integrate knowledge from a variety of sources. They are informed advocates for sound educational practices and policies.

While I reflect on my teaching after every lesson, viewing a videotape of my teaching gave me new perspectives into my teaching. My own and others' evaluations of my performance may not provide me with a complete view of the multiple interacting influences occurring in the classroom but a videotape of it provides a wider range of view that contains much objective information. I noticed aspects of the classroom environment, such as student engagement, that I wasn't fully aware of while teaching. I also noted other aspects of instruction, such as my behavior management strategies and tone of voice. This artifact fits under INTASC Principle 9 because I recognized my responsibility to engage in continual professional development. I combined my videotape observations with analysis of student work to evaluate my teaching. Throughout the reflection, I described ways in which I would revise my teaching practices to enhance student learning.

This artifact also meets NAEYC Principle 5 because I used a videotape in conjunction with my mentor's and my own observations to gain a comprehensive view of my work. I feel like a well-prepared teacher candidate because I allowed my practice to be influenced by knowledgeable, reflective, and critical perspectives. Observing myself on videotape provided me with a new perspective on my teaching. I found I was able to make adjustments to my lesson content, relationships with students, and classroom management to positively impact student learning.

Figure 7-11

Field Trip to Green Meadows Farm

INTASC Principle #10: Interpersonal relationships
The teacher fosters relationships with school colleagues, parents, and agencies in the larger community to support students' learning and well-being.

NAEYC Standard 4a: Connecting with children and families. Candidates know, understand, and use positive relationships and supportive interactions as the foundation for their work with young children.

This artifact, the result of a field trip planning experience, was completed by three student teachers placed in the same school. We worked together with our mentor teachers to complete all the necessary paperwork and steps in the planning stages of the field trip, and we were included in the actual field trip experience.

We placed this artifact under INTASC #10 and NAEYC Standard 4a because in planning the field trip we worked with each other, with our mentors, and with other school personnel as colleagues. We also worked with other agencies in the community arranging transportation with Green Meadows Farm and the bus company. We asked parents to volunteer to chaperone, and included as many as desired to come, because we felt the children would learn more from the experience in very small groups. Increased chaperon availability also ensured that the students had ample protection and support while on the trip. Additionally, welcoming parents on this field trip fostered positive relationships between the school, the parents, and the children in the classrooms. It gave parents an opportunity to meet each other and to feel more as if they were a part of the school community.

Activity 7-1

Go back to any of the ten examples, and identify the five components of a reflective narrative.
- Does it describe what the artifact is?
- Does it provide a clearly written rationale as to why the artifact was placed in the chosen INTASC/NAEYC Standards?
- Does this reflective narrative identify the writer's contribution to professional growth as an early childhood educator?
- Does the narrative describe how the artifact made a positive impact on student learning?
- Does the reflective narrative align itself within the core cluster of instructional activities?

Activity 7-2

Pick out one of your artifacts and write a reflective narrative, incorporating the five components. Have a classmate or instructor review your reflective narrative for clarity, written expression, and adherence to reflective narrative requirements.

Summary

You have learned in this chapter what a reflective narrative is and how to write a good one. You know that writing your narrative demands thought. Your narrative needs to extend your personal philosophy, provide a rationale for what you did and why you did it, clearly articulate why this artifact fits into the standard(s) you selected for it, and explain how it contributes to student learning and your own growth as a teacher. You know that it needs to include five components:

- What is the artifact?
- Why did I put it in this standard?
- How does this artifact contribute to my learning?
- How does this artifact contribute to student learning?
- Where does this artifact fit within the core cluster of activities in the classroom?

Remember that every narrative should not sound the same. Vary how you respond to the five necessary elements. There is no directive for the length of your narratives as long as you address the primary questions. However, a good rule of thumb is to keep your narrative to one page.

Suggested Web Sites

facstaff.uww.edu/eppsv/portfolio/portfolio_index.htm
e-Portfolio Information Part 3

References

Beck, I., McKeown, M.G., & Kucan. L. (2002). *Bring words to life: Robust vocabulary instruction*. New York: Guilford.

Model Standards for Beginning Teacher Licensing, Assessment and Development (1992) developed by Interstate New Teacher Assessment and Support Consortium. [On-line]
www.ccsso.org/content/pdfs/corestrd.pdf Accessed July 10, 2006.

CHAPTER 8

THE COLLECTION PHASE

Portfolios at academic institutions are often created as a part of a teacher preparation program. A purposeful collection of work that documents your experiences, activities, training, preparation, classroom skills, and accomplishments is an important part of building an effective portfolio. This important task involves gathering, sorting, and storing examples of what you are doing in college classes, in early childhood education settings, and what you have already done to illustrate your potential as a future early childhood educator. This chapter gives you suggestions about collecting, cataloging, and safely saving evidence that you might eventually use in your Showcase or Interview Portfolio.

How Does the Collection Phase Work?

Ideally, you should have begun collecting materials at the beginning of your journey toward becoming an early childhood teacher. You have already learned that this process is on going throughout your program. Looking back at the various types of portfolios defined in Chapter 1, the Collection, Developmental, and Assessment Portfolios could all be considered various levels of the gathering process, so an artifact you felt was appropriate as a freshman, may seem inappropriate as you mature and develop. However, at each level of your development, maybe at the end of each semester, collect and file evidence of your accomplishments, skills, assignments, internships, special training, journals, workshops, and other important activities in your life that pertain to your involvement with young children. We recommend that at this point you accumulate evidence from any of your classes, education, training, activities, hobbies, employment, and service that are relevant to you becoming a teacher. It is better to have too much, than too little. Save copies of your work, as well as backing up computer-generated documents. From this master collection, you will be able to select various artifacts for your Showcase Portfolio (Martin, 1999).

Collecting materials for an electronic portfolio is no different than amassing written materials, except that you want to save all files on a flash drive, DVD, or computer hard drive. It is wise to make back up copies of all the materials you prize.

What Artifacts Do I Want to Include?

Selection of artifacts for your portfolio in progress is an individual decision. This is where you can use your own creativity and sensitivity to decide what is important to showcase you as a future teacher. A list of possible artifacts is included on the next several pages with an explanation of each so that you may better facilitate their use. Each artifact is defined as it relates to early childhood education, and includes clarification about the skills and dispositions that it may encompass (Campbell et al., 2004).

You also may go back to Chapter 2 and view Figures 2-2, 2-3, and 2-4 and search the web for ideas of artifacts that are appropriate for a portfolio. Table 3-1 in Chapter 3 is a checklist to keep track of artifacts that you may have collected, and Table 3-2 provides possible artifacts that support each of the INTASC Principles and NAEYC Standards. These graphic organizers should be helpful in collecting, recording, and categorizing artifacts. Each time you add an artifact to your collection, it is wise to record the date and why you saved it (Martin, 1999).

Possible Portfolio Artifacts

Action research: Action research takes place in the classroom and is aimed at improving classroom instruction, student learning, or your own practice.

Anecdotal records: Notes taken during classroom observations or while teaching that may pertain to children's intellectual, social, physical, or emotional development; a valid assessment procedure in early childhood education.

Annotated bibliography: A study of children's literature and the criteria that make a quality book for 3- to 5-year-old children. Involves planning, diversity, and use of multiple resources.

Article summaries or critiques: A summary of an article in a professional journal is often a class assignment. When using it as a portfolio artifact, choose an article to critique that shows your ability to analyze professional material.

Assessments: Any artifact that measures children's performances would be considered assessment. Explain whether you are assessed children's performance, diagnosed progress, or used the assessment to modify instruction.

Attendance at PTA, school board meetings, or other school functions: Your own professional development is important. Attending school functions is a way to meet other professionals and families informally.

Attendance at conferences, workshops and/or seminars: Joining professional organizations, attending conferences, workshops and/or seminars provides opportunities to enhance your own professional development. Meeting other dedicated teachers and administrations in a professional setting, often provides you with new ideas and a fresh approach.

Author study: The study of one particular author over a period of time. Involves planning, implementing, and assessing student knowledge. Can provide motivation and use of a variety of resources to engage all learners.

Back-to-school night: A night when parents come to school to visit their children's classrooms and hear about the curriculum. This opportunity allows teachers to establish communication with families about procedures, routines, homework, and volunteering in the classroom.

Bulletin board displays: Creative displays showcasing children's work samples or highlighting a particular topic of interest or study. Can be used to motivate children, to collaborate with others, and to impact student learning.

Case study: A series of child observations focusing on one or more developmental domains usually documenting one child. This artifact shows knowledge of child development and could address typical or atypical development.

Child study: A series of reading and writing assessments about a child that provide information for daily instruction. An artifact that may help you understand diverse learners, child development, using assessment and differentiation to plan instruction.

Classroom management plan: A plan designed by the teacher to support student learning, instruction, behavior through documented routines and classroom procedures. Often this artifact falls under INTASC 5.

Community involvement: There are many ways to involve the community with academic activities and curriculum. Community resources can be used to foster student learning.

Conferencing with families: Parent-teacher conferences provide in-depth exchanges of information. While teachers can explain aspects of the curriculum, families can provide valuable information about children's special interests, concerns and background.

Computer programs analysis: An assignment that allows you to explore and analyze technology programs for young children. Involves knowledge of communication and technology, and could include specific ways to integrate technology in the classroom.

Content-specific units: Sometimes also know as themed units or projects, children's ideas and interests are investigated while teachers promote learning using organization, exploration, modeling, scaffolding, questioning, and documentation. These units show that children can reflect on what they have discovered.

Curriculum plans: Knowing the curriculum and planning daily, as well as long-term, are essential requirements for early childhood teachers. Connecting national, state, and local standards, and linking plans to children's prior knowledge are key concepts.

Cycle of learning: A two- or three-day (or longer) plan using one primary objective that is both measurable and observable. The cycle involves awareness of prior knowledge through the use of a pre-assessment, planning, teaching, both formative and summative assessment, analysis of data gathered, and reflection.

Ethics paper: Identifying an ethical issue or dilemma, familiarizing yourself with NAEYC's Code of Ethics, developing an action plan using the Code as your professional reference and citing specific ideals and principles from the Code to support your plan is the purpose of this artifact. Cite specific Ideals and Principles from the Code to support your plan. This artifact could perhaps illustrate collaboration, communication, and/or identification of professional literature to advance professional development and growth.

Field trip plans: Every community has endless possibilities for learning. Incorporating field trips can make learning real to children, but for field trips to be successful, advance planning and organization must take place.   This assignment involves planning, organization, and reflection.

Individual Education Plan: This is an assessment, intervention and evaluation plan designed with school staff to support children who need specific modifications in the daily instruction. IEPs involve administrators, specialists, families, as addition to the teacher and the child.

Integrating technology: Specifically designing lessons that integrate technology meaningfully in the classroom allow you to consult professionals who are knowledgeable about technology, as well as involve student in active, hand-on learning.

Journal entries: Journaling supports a reflective orientation that relates theory to practice. By continuously assessing one's teaching, considering a variety of viewpoints and perspectives, and understanding the personal, social, political, and moral implications of one's instruction decisions, journal entries should help you evaluate and reflect upon your teaching experiences, and chronicle your growth from student to pre-service teacher.

Lesson plans: A format or script that includes national, state, and local standards, goals and objectives, a list of materials, a list of procedures, closure, and assessments. This plan shows that you understand key ideas, methods of inquiry, content, students' developmental levels and student differences. Early childhood education lesson plans should be age- and developmentally appropriate.

Licensure or certification documentation: Standards in place by each state or district that provide requirements and certification or teachers and other professions in education. Documentation of licensure or certification indicates that you have met certain standards.

List of web sites: Making a list of web sites that will help you, as a teacher could be a viable artifact. Web sites can be found that include lesson plans, assessments, standards, newsletters, bulletin board ideas, and a variety of other viable topics.

Literacy bags: A bag of developmentally appropriate activities to support early literacy development at home. This activity encourages home-school connections.

Literacy study: Best practices in balanced reading instruction. A literacy study could involve planning, assessing, connecting with families, motivation, and integration with technology.

Newsletter: Regular written communication, in the native language of the family, that keeps families in touch with what is going on in the classroom.

Observations: Watching children in their school or child care environment for a specific purpose (example: to observe peer and caregiver interactions). There could be many reasons for observation such as collecting data, watching a specific child do a particular task, assessing, documenting developmental milestones, and designing instruction to meet individual needs.

Pacing guides: Instruction or curriculum guides that implement instruction in a particular sequence and/or a certain time frame. This might be one way to document efficient use of instructional time.

Parental involvement: Activities designed to build the home-school partnership and parent support from home. Many different artifacts could meet this goal.

Parent projects: Parent projects can vary from writing a newsletter to developing a home-school collaborative project. We know that when parents are involved in the learning process, children do better in school. This type of artifact provides effective communication between families and teachers to foster student learning and student success, and demonstrates professional use of oral and written language skills.

Peer critique: Feedback from peers during a supportive and cooperative critique of one's teaching that is focused on improving teaching and learning.

Philosophy of education statement: A statement of personal beliefs about how children learn and how you as an educator can support the development of the whole child. Shows your knowledge of content, child development, and ability to reflect.

Pre- and post-assessments: Used to assess children's prior knowledge before and after a unit of study or a lesson within a unit of study. Can be used to support how a lesson positively impacted student learning; can also be used to diagnose, monitor and evaluate progress.

Professional development plans: Individualized plans that support instruction specifically to improve the pedagogy of teachers. Could be used to assess your own development and/or to improve weak areas of the planning-teaching-assessing process.

Professional organization involvement: Joining and actively being involved in an organization that supports your professional interests and teaching. Many early childhood educators join NAEYC. Illustrates your participation in outside activities that could improve your practice.

Prop boxes: Integrated theme instruction with authentic, hands-on materials for a specific age group that will stimulate dramatic play, diversity, learning, and literacy development. This artifact could document your understanding of child development, connections to national, state, or local standards, a positive classroom environment, using a variety of materials to meet students' needs and helping students assume responsibility for their own learning.

Reflective writing: Similar to journals and self-evaluation, reflective writing allows you to combine educational theory with field experience teaching.

Research papers: Study and research related to a specific topic or learning domain.

Review an article from an early childhood journal: Shows use of professional literature, which could be done to develop professionally, to revise practice, to advance student learning, and/or to advance your own learning.

Samples of student work: Work samples document your ability to link student learning to prior knowledge, to meet students' needs, to encourage critical thinking and problem solving, to illustrate outcomes, and to document student achievement.

Samples of work showing a progression of ideas: Student work samples collected over time in a particular content area such as writing or math that can be used to plan and modify instruction.

Self-evaluation: Self-evaluation is a type of reflective practice asking you to describe and document your development during a particular time frame. It might ask you to relate back to course objectives to address your growth over time, or simply to evaluate a lesson/activity that you implemented in your field placement, identifying strengths and weaknesses in the lesson.

Service-Learning: Service-learning is a form of experiential education that involves a blending of community service activities with the academic curriculum. As you move from student to teacher, service-learning teaches responsibility, caring, giving, democratic character, integrity and authentic problem solving.

Teaching evaluations from mentors or supervisors: Evaluations from your mentor or your supervisor provides you with constructive feedback about all areas of teaching and learning.

Teacher-made materials: Materials could include, but are not limited to, games, manipulatives, puppets, books, charts, teaching aids, posters, and many more. Often these types of artifacts document active learning and using a variety of educational strategies.

Thematic units: Units of study designed around one theme, idea, or project that integrates many content areas. Use of this type of unit could illustrate long- and short-term planning, connecting national, state, and local standards to content, your ability to plan active and developmentally appropriate instruction, and the use of authentic assessment to document student learning.

Theme bags: Bags designed to support instructional themes through the use of hands-on activities. Often these bags are taken home; therefore, providing a home-school connection. They are also one way to document hands-one learning in various content areas.

Videotapes of you teaching: Videotaping is a tool to improve your teaching. It allows you to revisit your teaching and focus on a wider range of instructional decisions and student interactions with each repeated viewing. By viewing and critiquing yourself or others, you can reflect on the whole experience, and, as a result, develop a clearer sense of style, strengths, and areas for development.

Volunteer experience: This document could list and describe volunteer experience and service provided to a school and/or the community. Focus on the importance of the school-community connection and collaboration.

Sorting

Find a way to organize and categorize the documents that you have chosen to save. This task will be unique to you, as there are many ways you could do this. You may want to organize items around a theme, INTASC standards, content areas, grade level, chronologically by year or course. You may want to develop your own unique categories that are meaningful to you, like technology, group projects, educational theory, or lesson plans. No matter how you decide to organize your materials, keeping a checklist (see Table 3-1) of what you have is a good idea; this will allow you easy access to your artifacts.

Storing

Once again, how you choose to store your artifacts is up to you. To organize and store paper items, you might want to use pocket file folders, a file drawer, a large box, a file box or hanging files (Martin, 1999). No matter whether you are working on a paper or an electronic portfolio, it is wise to save clean copies of all your work, as well as backing up computer-generated documents.

Evaluating

Checklists and rubrics are popular and effective forms of assessment that help evaluators be objective and help students self-monitor (Bullock & Hawk, 2005; Rieman & Okrasinski, 2007). At this early phase of portfolio development, your work to date may be evaluated on content and organization. A rubric for those aspects might look something like what is detailed in Figure 8-1. Since portfolios are authentic products, the purposes of the rubric would be to show you where your strengths and areas for growth are at this point in time, and to promote an open dialogue between you and your professor about the current contents of your portfolio.

Figure 8-1   Pre-service Portfolio Sample Rubric

	1 **Indicator Not Met**	2 **Indicator Partially Met**	3 **Indicator Met**	4 **Indicator Met With Distinction**
Content				
INTASC Principles 1-10	Evidence demonstrates minimal or irrelevant knowledge of the principle.	There is evidence that some components of the principle are met.	The principle is met overall but some components may be more clearly met than others.	The principle is met through clear and consistent evidence showing comprehensive and explicit understanding.
Sources of evidence	Artifacts are not provided or are very similar	Artifacts show little variation.	Selected artifacts show some variety.	Wide variety of artifacts included.
Reflective narratives	Narratives are lacking necessary components and do not indicate that learning took place.	Narratives include some components and may or may not relate to the standard or what the intern has learned.	Narratives include all 5 components; overview of artifacts show a relationship to the standard and to what the intern has learned.	Narratives include all 5 components; overview of artifacts show a clear relationship to the standard and to what the intern has learned.
Philosophy Statement	Expresses little knowledge about child development and families.	Expresses some knowledge about child development and families	Expresses personal beliefs and knowledge about children and their families	Reflectively expresses personal beliefs and knowledge about children and their families
Organization	Portfolio lacks organization, is not systematically divided, and may confuse the reader.	Portfolio is somewhat organized, but may confuse the reader.	Portfolio is organized, divided systematically, and understandable.	Portfolio is logically organized, clearly divided systematically, and easily understood by any reader.
Artifacts	Not all three sections are included or completed.	Some sections are fully developed, but not all are.	Three sections are developed.	Three well-developed sections are included.

Figure 8-1   Pre-service Portfolio Sample Rubric, continued

	1 **Indicator Not Met**	2 **Indicator Partially Met**	3 **Indicator Met**	4 **Indicator Met With Distinction**
Appearance	Portfolio is neither professional nor neat.	Portfolio is somewhat professional and neat in appearance.	Portfolio is professional and neat in appearance.	Portfolio is professional in appearance and is visually pleasing.
Writing style	Artifacts are not professionally presented. Numerous errors.	Artifacts meet most standards for professional presentation. Some errors in spelling or grammar.	Professionally presented using clean copies; grammatically correct, spell checked. Few errors.	Professionally presented using clean copies; grammatically correct, spell checked, and creatively presented.

Another tool you could use is a checklist for evaluating an INTASC Standard Portfolio. For each of the INTASC Principles, you could develop a simple check system.

_____ My evidence matches the principle.

_____ My reflection shows a clear relationship to the principle.

_____ The INTASC principle is met. (Bullock & Hawk, 2005).

Activity 8-1

Use Figure 8-2 to chart and categorize the artifacts you have collected to date. Be cognizant of having a variety of artifacts.

Figure 8 –2
Chart for collecting and categorizing artifacts

Assignment or Experience	Date	INTASC Principle met

Summary

The collection phase includes the gathering, sorting, and safely storing of materials amassed during your undergraduate course work. Even if particular courses or instructors do not require specific artifacts for the Professional Portfolio, it is important that you continue to add and organize evidence from your course work and internship experiences. Remember that the collection phase is an ongoing process.

Suggested Web Sites

INTASC portfolio development. http://www.ccsso.lorg/projects/
Penn State's Center for Excellence in Teaching and Learning. http://www.psu.edu/celt/portfolio.html.
http://www.uwrf.edu/ccs.portfolio-steps.htm

References

Bullock, A. A., & Hawk, P. P. (2005). *Developing a teaching portfolio: A guide for preservice and practicing teachers* (2nd ed.). Upper Saddle River, NJ: Merrill/Prentice Hall.

Campbell, D. M., Cignetti, P. B., Melenyzer, B. J., Nettles, D. H., & Wyman, R. M. (2007). *How to develop a professional portfolio: A manual for teachers* (4th ed.). Boston: Allyn & Bacon.

Martin, D. B. (1999). *The portfolio planner: Making professional portfolios work for you.* Upper Saddle River, NJ: Prentice Hall.

Rieman, P., & Okrasinski, J. (2007). *Creating your teaching portfolios* (2nd ed.). New York: McGraw Hill.

CHAPTER 9

THE SELECTION PHASE:

CHOOSING ARTIFACTS FOR THE SHOWCASE PORTFOLIO

You have developed a large, viable collection of artifacts. Your job now is to refine them into a polished, balanced Showcase Portfolio. You must decide which samples best illustrate important insights, accomplishments, beliefs, and values, and then consider how to use them to present yourself to an audience as a skilled early childhood candidate who meets all INTASC Principles and NAEYC Core Standards (Martin, 1999). Your portfolio is evidence of your learning and growth throughout your undergraduate early childhood program. Your portfolio should include your personal documents (see Chapter 3 for a review), the professional background section that illustrates your understanding of what it means to be a teacher of young children, and any supplemental artifacts that might be included in the Appendix. All of your examples should now be of the highest quality. This chapter looks at ways to help you select the most appropriate examples of the work you have done.

How Do I Select What is Best from My Collection of Artifacts?

As you have been developing and working on your portfolio throughout your program, you have undoubtedly had feedback and constructive criticism from professors and instructors. In every class you have taken, you have received indication of work that is of the highest quality. This is what you want to include in your Showcase Portfolio.

You might consult peers, mentor teachers, or people outside the education field to look over your final choices. Certainly, those familiar with INTASC principles and NAEYC standards can give you advice and opinions about what they think should be included. But parents and friends who are not teachers can also proofread and give you an outsider's opinion.

As you progress in your program, your courses focus almost exclusively on early childhood education and you are engaged in longer and more extensive field placements. These two components help you acquire and apply knowledge of developmental theory, curricular content, learning styles, diversity, technology, planned instruction, classroom organization and management, formal and informal assessment, and professional development. At the heart of the selection process is identifying documentation of best practices, developmentally appropriate active learning, and well-written reflections. These documents will result in an authentic assessment medium—your portfolio. As you engage in your final capstone experience, often known as student teaching, you take on increased responsibilities for teaching in diverse, inclusive, and technologically advanced environments.

The final requirement for graduation at many institutions is the completed Showcase Portfolio, presented to a panel of teachers, administrators, and/or faculty during their final semester. This sharing is a powerful culminating activity whereby interns celebrate the importance of their work with seasoned professionals who provide them feedback.

While all portfolios create a context for feedback about teaching experiences, the Showcase Portfolio provides helpful formative assessment and an excellent tool for self-evaluation because it promotes reflecting on goals, areas of strength and areas for growth, and developing rationales for the chosen selections. Summative assessment purposes and benefits include presenting a personal portrait of yourself, chronicling your professional development, tailoring your presentation to the use of specific standards, using multiple sources of evidence, and providing evidence over time that the standards have been met.

Electronic portfolios allow you to capture and store information in the form of documents, spreadsheets, databases, photographs of projects, voice recordings of oral skills such as reading, speaking, and singing, video recordings of teaching sequences, QuickTimeVR movies, and multimedia projects of web pages exploring curriculum topics, currents events, or ethical questions. This capability enables you to produce a multimedia portrayal of your skills and accomplishments (Pollard, 2006; http:///www.schools.pinellas.k12.fl.us/itu/classfive/Lesson5.2.html).

Suggestions for Success

- Balance the collection of artifacts so that all 10 INTASC principles have approximately the same number of artifacts. For the Showcase Portfolio, 3-5 artifacts per principle are recommended.
- Choose only your very best work.
- Lead each section with your strongest artifacts.
- Use good quality paper that has a professional look.
- Be consistent in style, type, and paper.
- Strive for a visual identity.
- Select recent and relevant examples.
- Include student work samples, especially with lesson plans and assessments.
- Use only clean copies.
- Put each page of the artifact/assignment in clear plastic sheet protectors.
- Use a variety of artifacts.
- Vary the reflective narratives.
- Include samples of technological competence.
- Strive for neatness and careful organization.
- Spell check and proofread everything.

Activity 9-1

Refer to Figure 7-1. The criteria should be your guide for choosing your best artifacts that showcase your professional growth and learning.

Summary

A Showcase Portfolio "is compiled for the expressed purpose of giving others an effective and easy-to-read portrait of your professional competence" (Campbell et al, 2004, p. 4). As you present this work as a summative evaluation prior to graduation, you demonstrate the nature and quality of your day-to-day work. This evidence goes far beyond what words on a resume do. It sets you apart as a unique individual whose work depicts the knowledge, skills, dispositions, and attitudes necessary to successfully succeed as a teacher of young children.

Suggested Web Sites

This site provides a guideline for choosing possible artifacts and how to present your work.
www.midsolutions.org .

http:///www.schools.pinellas.k12.fl.us/itu/classfive/Lesson5.2.html

References

Campbell, D. M., Cignetti, P. B., Melenyzer, B. J., Nettles, D. H., & Wyman, R. M. (2007). *How to develop a professional portfolio: A manual for teachers* (4th ed.). Boston: Allyn & Bacon.

Martin, D. B. (1999). *The portfolio planner: Making professional portfolios work for you.* Upper Saddle River, NJ: Prentice Hall.

Pollard, R. R. (2006). *Showcasing new teachers: Electronic portfolios.* [On-line] Available at www.ictge.org/T01_Library/T01_140.pdf. Retrieved January 17, 2007.

http:///www.schools.pinellas.k12.fl.us/itu/classfive/Lesson5.2.html [On-line] Retrieved May 23, 2007.

CHAPTER 10

THE FINAL PHASE:

PREPARING, ASSESSING, AND PRESENTING YOUR PORTFOLIO

The best methods of preparation for the summative portfolio review is through peer evaluations, conferencing with your university instructor(s), mock interviews, and familiarity with your final professional portfolio. Once again, this involves on-going reflection and analysis. Your portfolio is a working document, requiring continuous reflection. The more time you spend preparing for the portfolio evaluation, the more comfortable you will become with the INTASC Principles and NAEYC Standards. You will also need to be able to articulate how well your individual artifacts demonstrate your understanding of the educational principles and practices in dealing with young children and their families.

The portfolio review and presentation is a powerful tool for the pre-service intern, as well as for the assessors. It illustrates tangible evidence of your ability to take on the responsibility of teaching and caring for young children. The goal of this chapter is to help you prepare and present your professional portfolio as both a summative evaluation of your pre-service teaching career and as a preparation for the interview process.

Preparing for the Presentation

Once you have collected an adequate number of artifacts, it is time to thoughtfully evaluate each one to make sure it best exemplifies the INTASC Principle it has been chosen to represent. While there is no definitive number of artifacts required, we recommend that you have a balanced number of artifacts in each of the ten INTASC principles, probably between 3 and 5 per standard. Include evidence from a variety of sources that best represent you as a teacher and learner. Try to include artifacts from many content areas (reading, language arts, mathematics, science, social studies, technology, art, music and movement). While one artifact may reflect more than one INTASC Principle, try to use it only once. Reflection is critical in the self-examination and growth process. Use reflection to clearly portray your experience of becoming a teacher.

Evaluating Your Professional Portfolio

Assessing a professional portfolio can be done using a variety of methods. While you are still in the initial stage of your professional development, it is expected that some of your artifacts will be from your coursework. However, there must also be documentation that provides evidence that you are a successful practitioner. Furthermore, authentication of positive effects and outcomes on student learning and how that affects future planning for children, is imperative. If you are about to graduate from an accredited teacher education program your portfolio development may be tied to graduation requirements, program guidelines, or specific criteria such as INTASC Principles and NAEYC Standards. Using a checklist like Figure 10-1 will allow you to be sure that all required materials are included.

Figure 10-1   Professional Portfolio Checklist

_____ Appropriate container

_____ Cover page

_____ Table of contents

_____ Philosophy statement

_____ Personal data

_____ Resume

_____ Transcripts

_____ INTASC Principles 1-10

_____ Each section is clearly marked and accessible.

_____ Each section contains at least 2-3 artifacts.

_____ Each artifact is preceded by a reflective narrative.

_____ Student work is included to support at least some artifacts.

_____ Photographs are used to strengthen artifacts.

_____ All student identification is removed.

_____ Clean copies of work are used.

_____ Material is placed in plastic sheet protectors for a paper portfolio.

_____ All work is free of grammatical, spelling, and punctuation errors.

Figure 10-2 is a 5-point rubric using the INTASC Principles and NAEYC Standards that could be used to appraise the Professional Portfolio. We recommend that a minimum score of 3 be required on each of the 10 INTASC Principles. At our institution, program completion is delayed for interns who do not attain a 3 or above until revision of the artifact and/or reflective narrative is completed to reach at least the basic level.

In Figure 10-2, each numbered INTASC Principle found in column 1 represents the overall objective of the principle. The bulleted items in column 2 represent the indicators for that principle. Critically evaluate your artifacts, and ask yourself, do the artifacts selected address each one of the bulleted indicators? For example, in INTASC #5, you need to demonstrate your understanding of motivation and classroom management. Many pre-service interns explain their competence in this area by using a lesson plan that they felt was motivating for children. But, did you include an artifact and the accompanying reflective narrative that demonstrates that you devised and enacted a classroom management plan that provided a positive learning environment? (Indicator 1). Did you document strategies used to engage students in active learning? (Indicator 2). How did you encourage students to assume responsibility for their own learning? (Indicator 3). Can you show how you efficiently used instructional time? (Indicator 4). Did you include an artifact that documents collaboration with team members, administrators, and/or parents to promote positive behavior? (Indicator 5). It's important to meet each indicator, as well as the overall objective.

You may need to add new artifacts or refine your reflective narratives to directly include each indicator. By reshaping individual artifacts to better fit the indicators under each INTASC principle, you clarify your own understanding. Decide where you need to add or delete artifacts, if you need to move artifacts from one INTASC principle to another, or if you have reflective narratives that need fine-tuning.

Figure 10-2   Portfolio Assessment Rubric

INTASC Principles NAEYC Core Standards	Indicators	Scoring 5 Distinguished 4 Proficient 3 Basic 2 Needs improvement 1 Unsatisfactory

1. Knowledge of subject matter
    4b. Using developmentally effective approaches
    4c. Understanding content knowledge in early education
    4d. Building meaningful curriculum
	• Connections to the national/state/local standards of the discipline
	• Focused instruction on key ideas and methods of inquiry in the discipline
	• Content linked to students' prior understandings
		5 Knowledge of content is met through comprehensive, clear, and consistent evidence; each indicator is met fully.
		
		4 Content is good, but some indicators may be more clearly met than others.
		
		3 Evidence for content and reflection met.
		
		2 Evidence of some understanding of content. Reflections do not clearly articulate how the standard is met.
		
		1 Minimal or irrelevant understanding of content. Reflections do not articulate how the standard is met.

2. Knowledge of human development
    1. Promoting child development and learning
    4b. Using developmentally effective approaches
    4d. Building meaningful curriculum
	• Knowledge of typical and atypical growth and development
	•Instruction designed to meet learner's current need based on age, development, learning style, readiness, ability, culture, social group and/or values.
		5 Knowledge of child development is met through comprehensive, clear, and consistent evidence; each indicator is met fully.
		
		4 Knowledge of child development is met using evidence; each indicator is met.
		
		3 Knowledge of child development is met; most indicators are met.
		
		2 Knowledge of child development is not met consistently; some indicators are met.
		
		1 Knowledge of child development is lacking. Few indicators are met.

Figure 10-2   Portfolio Assessment Rubric, continued

INTASC Principles NAEYC Core Standards	Indicators	Scoring **5 Distinguished** **4 Proficient** **3 Basic** **2 Needs improvement** **1 Unsatisfactory**
3. Instruction adapted for diverse learners 1. Promoting child development and learning 2. Building family and community relationships 4b. Using developmentally effective approaches	• Differentiated instruction for divers and inclusive community of learners/students (e.g., diversity factors include but are not limited to race, ethnicity, religion, region, gender, language, SES, age, and individuals with exceptionalities or learning styles) • Evidence of multiple perspectives in subject matter	**5** Evidence that instruction can be adapted for diverse learners is met through comprehensive, clear, and consistent evidence; each indicator is met fully. **4** Evidence that instruction can be adapted for diverse learners is met; each indicator is met. **3** Evidence that instruction can be adapted for diverse learners is met; most indicators are met. **2** Evidence that instruction adapted for diverse learners is weak. **1** Evidence that instruction for diverse learners is poor or nonexistent.
4. Use of multiple strategies and resources 4b. Using developmentally effective approaches 4d. Building meaningful curriculum	• Variety of instructional strategies (including assessment) to achieve different purposes and meet students' needs • Instruction encouraging critical thinking/problem solving	**5** Use of many teaching strategies and a variety of resources demonstrated comprehensively; each indicator is met fully. **4** Use of multiple teaching strategies and a variety of resources is met; each indicator is met, some more completely than others. **3** Use of teaching strategies and resources is met; most indicators are met. **2** Some teaching strategies and resources are demonstrated. **1** Few teaching strategies and resources are demonstrated.

Figure 10-2   Portfolio Assessment Rubric, continued

INTASC Principles NAEYC Core Standards	Indicators	Scoring 5 Distinguished 4 Proficient 3 Basic 2 Needs improvement 1 Unsatisfactory
5. Learning environment/motivation and behavior 1. Promoting child development and learning 3. Observing, documenting, and assessing to support young children and families 4b. Using developmentally effective approaches 4d. Building meaningful curriculum	• Classroom management plan provides a positive, productive learning environment • Strategies to engage students in active learning • Encouragement of students' assuming responsibility for their own learning • Efficient use of instructional time • Collaboration with team members, administrators, and parents to promote positive behavior	**5** Organization and management of a classroom is met through outstanding evidence; each indicator is met fully. **4** Evidence of organization and management of a classroom is met; each indicator is met. **3** Evidence of organization and management of a classroom is clearly met; most indicators are met. **2** Organization and management of a classroom is not clearly demonstrated; some indicators are met. **1** Organization and management of a classroom is not demonstrated; few indicators are met.
6. Effective communication 4a. Connecting with children and families 4b. Using developmentally effective approaches	• Demonstration of professional use of oral and written language skills • Integrated instructional application of appropriate technologies • Application of technology to meet professional needs.	**5** Effective use of professional oral and written language and application of technology is evident throughout. **4** Use of professional oral and written language and application of technology is consistent throughout. **3** Use of professional oral and written language and application of technology is provided. **2** Professional oral and written language and application of technology is sometimes evident. **1** Neither professional oral and written language nor application to technology are substantiated.

Figure 10-2   Portfolio Assessment Rubric, continued

INTASC Principles NAEYC Core Standards	Indicators	Scoring 5 Distinguished 4 Proficient 3 Basic 2 Needs improvement 1 Unsatisfactory
7. Planning for instruction 1. Promoting child development and learning 2. Building family and community relationships 3. Observing, documenting, and assessing to support young children and families 4a. Connecting with children and families 4b. Using developmentally effective approaches 4d. Building meaningful curriculum	• Creation of daily and long-term plans aligned with national/state/local curriculum goals, students' needs and prior knowledge and strategies for active learning • Use of assessment data to adjust instruction	**5** Planning for instruction is met through lesson plans, assessments, and student work samples. Use of curriculum goals and assessment data is documented fully and completely. **4** Planning for instruction is met. Use of curriculum goals and assessment data is documented. **3** Planning for instruction is met. Most indicators are met. Use of curriculum goals and assessment data is documented. **2** Planning for instruction is sometimes met. Use of curriculum goals and assessment data is unclear or missing. **1** Planning for instruction is weak; use of curriculum goals and assessment data is missing.
8. Assessment of student learning 3. Observing, documenting, and assessing to support young children and families.	• Use of assessment plan to demonstrate positive impact on student learning • Use of pre and post-assessments as well as formative assessment to diagnose, monitor, and document student progress • Use of information obtained from review of student work to plan and modify instruction	**5.** A variety of assessments are used consistently including pre- and post-data to improve instruction. **4** Pre- and post- assessments are used consistently, as are other assessments. All indicators are met. **3** Pre- and post- assessments are used; all indicators are met. **2** Little variety in assessments used. Pre- and post- assessments rarely used. **1** No variety; pre- and post-assessments are not used.

Figure 10-2   Portfolio Assessment Rubric, continued

INTASC Principles NAEYC Core Standards	Indicators	Scoring 5 Distinguished 4 Proficient 3 Basic 2 Needs improvement 1 Unsatisfactory
9. Professional growth and reflection 5. Becoming a professional	• Integration of classroom observation and analysis of data about students to evaluate the outcomes of teaching and to revise practice • Consultation of professional literature, colleagues, and other professional learning opportunities to advance student learning • Evidence of positive impact of professional development of student achievement	**5** Professional growth is obvious; Reflections show comprehensive, understanding; each indicator is met fully. **4** Professional growth is clear. Reflections show understanding; each indicator is met. **3** Professional growth and reflection is evident. **2** Reflections do not indicate substantial professional growth. **1** Minimal or no professional growth illustrated.

10. Interpersonal relationships
   2. Building family and community relationships
   4a. Connecting with children and families
   5. Becoming a professional
	• Participation in collegial activities, directed at the improvement of teaching and learning.
	• Effective communication with families, teachers, resource personnel to foster student learning and success
	• Identification and use of community resources to foster student learning and success
		5 Interpersonal relationships with colleagues, families, and children are documented fully; each indicator is met fully.
		
		4 Interpersonal relationships with colleagues, families, and children are documented; most indicators are met.
		
		3 Interpersonal relationships with colleagues, families, and children are documented; some indicators are met.
		
		2 Interpersonal relationships with colleagues, families, and children are not well documented; few indicators are met.
		
		1 Interpersonal relationships with colleagues, families, and children are not documented.

(Department of Early Childhood Education, Towson University)

Figure 10-3 is a 4-point rubric for scoring electronic portfolios that includes items related to media design as well as content and professionalism (midsolutions.org). This sample is included for institutions using electronic portfolios. Adapted from Rieman and Okrasinski (2007), Figure 10-4 is an Oral Presentation Rubric that might also be a useful assessment tool for oral presentations.

Figure 10-3   Electronic Portfolio Assessment Rubric

	Needs Improvement 0-2 points	Basic 3 points	Proficient 4 points	Distinguished 5 points
Media and Design Elements				
Typography	Subheadings, titles, and text are displayed in sizes that are inconsistent with content hierarchy. Excessive scrolling exists. Numerous font styles are utilized, increasing file size.	Subheadings, titles, and text are displayed in the same size. Some large blocks of text are used. Variety of font styles are used to enhance design.	Subheadings, titles, and text are displayed in sizes that reflect content hierarchy; few blocks of text exist. Some inconsistencies in of font styles.	Subheadings, titles, and text are displayed in sizes that reflect content hierarchy; avoided excessive scrolling in text blocks. Minimal number of font styles utilized.
Images	Some images are appropriate for the content and have few if any alterative text (ALT tags).	Most images are appropriate and several have alternative text (ALT tags). Not all images are displayed with appropriate sizing and resolution.	All images are appropriate for the content and target audience. All have alternative text (ALT tags). Images are displayed with appropriate sizing and resolution.	All images are appropriate for the content and target audience. Informative alternative text (ALT tags) are supplied for all graphics. All images are displayed with appropriate sizing and resolution.
Audio & Video	Contains inappropriate or no digitized audio and video artifacts.	Incorporates one or two digitized audio and video artifacts.	Incorporates appropriate digitized audio and video artifacts.	Effectively incorporates digitized audio and video artifacts.
Layout	Layout follows a consistent pattern; does not reflect the purpose of the content or the needs of the target audience.	Layout follows a consistent pattern, reflects the purpose of the content but does not address a specific audience.	Layout follows a consistent pattern and reflects the purpose of the content.	Layout follows a consistent pattern, reflects the purpose of the content and is targeted for a specific audience.

Figure 10-3   Electronic Portfolio Assessment Rubric, continued

	Needs Improvement 0-2 points	Basic 3 points	Proficient 4 points	Distinguished 5 points
Hyperlinks	Most internal and external hyperlinks are appropriate for the content; some function incorrectly.	Most internal and external hyperlinks are appropriate for the content, function correctly.	Most internal and external hyperlinks are appropriate for the content, function correctly, and are appropriate for a general audience.	Internal and external hyperlinks are appropriate for the content, function correctly, and are for a specific targeted audience.
Navigation	Difficult to navigate. Navigations bar is missing or is inappropriate for the content and/or design.	Fairly easy to navigate. The navigation bar is inconsistent across the product or is missing in certain areas.	Easy to navigate. Navigation bar is included and consistent across the product. Navigation bar assists viewer in finding specific data.	Easy to navigate. Navigation bar is included and consistent across the product. Navigation bar assists viewer in finding specific data. Designed for a specific target audience.
Audience	Artifacts address some standards and Department of Education requirements.	Artifacts address standards, Department of Education requirements, and fit the purpose of a general audience.	Artifacts address standards, Department of Education requirements, and fit the purpose and usefulness of a generic audience.	Artifacts clearly address standards, Department of Education requirements, and fit the purpose and usefulness of a specific audience.
Content				
Thoroughness	Artifacts are poor in quality and some competencies are not addressed. Rationales are weak or missing.	Artifacts to demonstrate learning outcomes for some standards. Artifacts are of a basic quality. Rationales are weak.	Sufficient number of artifacts to demonstrate learning outcomes for each standard. Artifacts are of a good quality and include a rationale.	Sufficient number of artifacts to demonstrate learning outcomes for each standard. Artifacts are of a high quality and include a well-stated rationale.

Figure 10-3   Electronic Portfolio Assessment Rubric, continued

	Needs Improvement 0-2 points	Basic 3 points	Proficient 4 points	Distinguished 5 points
Reflections; rationale	Reflections are unclear or missing.	Incomplete or general artifact reflections are provided.	Appropriate reflections for each artifact are included.	Appropriate and complete reflections are included for each artifact.
Evidence of learning	Unclear or contradictory evidence of growth and professional practice missing.	Evidence of growth and of improvement in professional practice is basic.	Clear evidence of growth; general evidence of improvement in professional practice included.	Consistent evidence of growth; improvement in professional practice is clear.
Professional philosophy	Professional philosophy is unclear or contradictory.	Professional philosophy is described, but no justifications for beliefs are included.	Professional philosophy is described; general justifications for beliefs are included.	Professional philosophy is clearly described and includes specific and appropriate references to justify beliefs.
Background information	Resume, educational goals and philosophy are unclear or missing.	Current resume, educational goals, and philosophy are included, but may be unclear.	Current resume, generic educational philosophy and professional goals are included.	Current resume, clearly defined educational philosophy, and professional goals are included.
Professionalism				
Professional development plan	Weak or no professional development plan is provided.	Non-specific plan for professional development; no efforts to improve practice are identified.	Plan for professional development, and ideas for refining practice are general.	Plan describes specific methods of continually refining professional practice.
Innovation	Strategies for classroom practice or ideas for multimedia projects are either inappropriate or missing.	One-two general strategies for practice are included. Inappropriate multimedia projects.	New strategies for classroom practice are provided. Multimedia projects included.	New strategies for classroom practice and many multimedia projects for classroom use are provided.

(Adapted from https://midsolutions.org/portfolios/assessments.htm)

Figure 10-4

Oral Presentation Rubric

	Unsatisfactory 0-2 points	Basic 3 points	Proficient 4 points	Distinguished 5 points
Content	Content is not clearly presented; information does not support the standards.	Content is presented with some supporting details.	Content and many supporting details are presented.	Abundance of interesting details to support content is presented.
Organization	Presentation is disjointed and unorganized.	Presentation is organized.	Presentation is well organized.	Well-developed introduction, body of information, and conclusion presented.
Speaking skills	No eye contact shown. Delivery is too fast or too slow; voice is a monotone.	Presentation is good, but lacks confidence and eye contact with assessors.	Articulate delivery style is used, including good eye contact throughout the presentation.	Articulate, energetic, poised, confident delivery style is used. Excellent eye contact is maintained.
Audience response	Audience loses interest and/or cannot follow the content presented.	Audience is interested, but information is not compelling.	Audience is attentive throughout the presentation.	Audience is attentive and interested throughout the presentation.

(Adapted from Rieman & Okrasinski, 2007)

Examine the evaluation rubrics provided in this chapter or ones provided by your college or university to self-evaluate your work to date. Working with evaluation rubrics is apt to improve your understanding of the principles used to judge your portfolio.

Peer Evaluation

Ask your classmates, university supervisors, mentor teachers, and instructors to look over your portfolio to provide you with feedback. If you struggle with written expression, grammar, and spelling, make sure you have a classmate, family member, or friend check it for you. You may have a thoughtful, complete portfolio but if it is full of errors, the errors are what assessors focus on, and the question is raised, "Is this pre-service intern a professional ready to take on the responsibility of teaching in an early childhood setting?" Your portfolio is the tangible representation of you as a pre-service teacher.

In our program, some instructors do peer reviewing as an in-class activity learning tool. Having the opportunity to look at other portfolios can help you with your own portfolio. Your classmates may have included artifacts in their portfolios that you had not even considered using; they may have placed artifacts under INTASC principles that you had not contemplated. Look at and evaluate as many portfolios as you possibly can, as you will grow and learn from each experience. Some instructors actually periodically grade and give constructive criticism on portfolio progress at various stages. Ask your mentor, university supervisor, or instructor to look over your portfolio to provide you with feedback. Frequently, these educational professionals can provide you with practical suggestions and guidance. This is also an opportunity for you to "strut your stuff," as a well-thought-out and organized portfolio clearly exemplifies your professional attributes.

Portfolio Defense

Prior to the portfolio review procedures used by your college or university, set-up a mock portfolio interview as a practice session. For the practice mock interview, have one classmate sit on one side of the table, with his or her portfolio and additional classmates play the role of assessors. Allow for time for the intern to present an introductory statement, and then have the assessment panel ask questions of the intern from the provided list. Allow enough time for all class members to sit in the "hot seat." Practicing the portfolio assessment process helps you prepare for the actual interview and provides you with possible and probable questions that may arise during the actual portfolio review. Many of these same questions may also be asked during interviews for teaching positions.

The Actual Presentation

The night of your presentation has come! You are excited, but nervous. As you approach the assessors, take a deep breath! At our institution, the assessment panel is comprised of one university faculty member and two other educational professionals, often mentor teachers or administrators from our Professional Development Schools. All are dedicated persons with a strong understanding of our departmental standards and procedures, and the INTASC Principles and NAEYC Standards. They understand the skills, attributes, and dispositions of an early childhood professional.

Remember, the best portfolio in the world won't help you if you don't know how to use it. Let it help you respond to the assessors' questions. If an assessor asks you for an example of a time when a certain skill failed you, do not stress out. No one expects you to be perfect, but the assessors may want to see how you handle yourself. Give an example, but be sure to point out what you learned from the experience and how you would handle the situation now.

Before the actual presentation, you will have practiced presenting your portfolio to peers, your advisor, or another faculty member. Figure 10-5 provides a list of sample interview questions that you can read ahead of time and think about. The presentation of your professional portfolio prepares you well for up-coming interviews with principals and school system officials.

Figure 10-5   Sample Interview Questions

Sample Interview Questions

How did you decide what artifacts to include in your portfolio?
What would you consider your strengths? What evidence in your portfolio supports your these strengths?
Did the majority of your artifacts come from your internship experiences?
How will you be able to use your portfolio in the classroom?
What do you consider the most important artifacts in your portfolio?
Describe your learning that took place while creating your portfolio.
What is your philosophy of education?
What is the purpose of your portfolio?
Which lessons included in your portfolio did students most enjoy?
What artifact best represents you?
Which INTASC Principle is your strongest? What INTASC Principle would you like to investigate and support more?
What part of your portfolio was the most difficult to prepare?
How does your portfolio support your growth as a teacher?
In your opinion, what INTASC Principle is most important?
Describe a specific lesson that describes your beliefs as an educator.
What classroom management strategies have you successfully implemented?
How do you show children you care?
Describe how you incorporated NAEYC Standards in your teaching.
What did you learn about yourself as you assembled your portfolio?
What did you learn about yourself while you worked in classrooms with young children?
What is the most significant experience you will take into your own classroom?

Suggestions for a Successful Presentation

- **Know your portfolio!** Consider making a copy of your table of contents so that during the portfolio review, you have a quick reference to where artifacts are in your portfolio. Use your artifacts to support your verbal response to questions.

- **Know your audience.** Be knowledgeable about current "hot" issues in education and be able to articulate non-biased, research-based understandings.

- **Dress for success**. Consider this a job interview and dress for the part. Wear clothing that is professional, relatively conservative, and comfortable.

- **Start off on the right foot**. Practice a firm handshake, making eye contact, and have a brief planned introductory statement to avoid an awkward silence.

- **Answer the question.** Try to provide a direct, concise answer to a direct question and use the artifacts of your portfolio as tangible support. Allow the portfolio assessors time to ask the necessary questions.

Activity 10-1

Plan a mock interview with peers, instructors, and supervisors. Provide your mock assessors with questions as a guideline. Practice defending your work and presenting your portfolio as a teaching professional.

Summary

You have carefully prepared for this event. Your care in developing your Showcase Portfolio has demanded your time, energy, and careful reflection. You know your portfolio better than anyone; therefore, your presentation will be unique because it reflects your abilities, strengths, creativity, and professionalism. Confidence is the key to making a good impression. Know yourself. Present your achievements succinctly, and use your portfolio to provide concrete examples that clearly demonstrate your skills and your strengths. Good luck!

Suggested Web Sites

The Delta Program is dedicated to research in teacher preparation. This web site serves as a guide book to prepare in preparing a professional portfolio at www.delta.wisc.edu.

A manual from the University of Wisconsin—River Falls—provides a general sequence in beginning and maintaining a professional portfolio. www.uwrf.edu

UMD Career Services *Career handbook* (7th ed.) includes interviewing tips and questions for teacher candidates. http://careers.d.umn.edu/cs_handbook/cshandbook_interviewing.html.

References

Career handbook (7th ed). Electronic Portfolio Assessment Rubric [On-line] https://midsolutions.org/portfolios/assessments.htm Retrieved May 23, 2007.

Portfolio assessment rubric. (2006). Department of Early Childhood Education, Towson University, Towson, MD.

Rieman, P. L., & Okrasinski, J. (2007). *Creating your teaching portfolio* (2nd ed.). Boston: McGraw Hill.

CHAPTER 11

TAKING YOUR PORTFOLIO TO THE NEXT STEP

Thus far, you have learned that the purpose of the portfolio is to document your professional growth and competence in the complex act of teaching through an organized collection of artifacts that begins when you enter college and continues throughout your entire program. Course assignments such as writing and implementing lesson plans, planning field trips, implementing service-learning projects, engaging in action research, and participating in school improvement teams add value to teacher preparation, and often serve as viable artifacts. But what happens now? In this final chapter, we look at how your portfolio has prepared you to interview for potential teaching positions and enter the work force as a professional in the field of early childhood education.

Preparation Before the Interview

Keys to successful interviewing include knowing yourself. Present yourself as someone who has something to offer this particular school system or school. Know as much about the school system, the school, and the requirements of the job as you can. Arrive at the interview early. Dress appropriately. Bring an interview portfolio with you. By having your Interview Portfolio handy, you will be able to provide concrete examples that demonstrate your skills, knowledge and attitudes related to teaching. Get a good night's sleep, be well rested, and alert. Practice answering questions that you think will be asked by the interviewer or interview team.

The Interview Portfolio

Your Interview Portfolio is the probably the most important marketing tool you will ever create. Take the time and effort necessary to develop one that represents you. Using your Showcase Portfolio, or any other artifacts that you have saved, prepare a portfolio specifically designed for a particular interview. For example, let's say you are applying for a kindergarten position at your desired school. Put together personal documents that include a letter of introduction, a resume, university transcripts, Praxis I and II scores, a philosophy statement, and one or two letters of recommendation. Then include several artifacts that were specifically planned for kindergarten-level children. This could include, but is not limited to, lesson plans, work samples, and appropriate assessments. A wise choice would be to include a lesson plan with a reflection about your teaching effectiveness, documentation of student learning, and data to support it. Perhaps you will want to include a lesson where you adapted instruction to meet the needs of all students. Select the best and most relevant of the documents. Use copies rather than originals.

The interviewer wants to gather as much relevant information about you as he or she can, to assess how well your qualifications match the requirements of the position. When you have a portfolio with you, the interviewer can determine how well your portfolio artifacts relate to his or her needs (Kimeldorf, 1997). Sometimes interns complain that the interviewer "never looked at my portfolio." If you bring a busy principal a 3-inch binder with 30 artifacts, many times he or she couldn't possibly look at it carefully. Be wise. Be brief. Do not bring a massive portfolio with you to interviews. Your final Interview Portfolio probably should not exceed 25 pages, and shorter is better (Kimeldorf, 1997). Be highly selective and include only the most essential documents relevant to the position for which you are applying.

An interview portfolio is an asset. Some candidates create a small version of their portfolio that can be left with the interviewer. This can be a copied version that includes of a small sampling of documents. Other interviewees develop a brochure that provides interviewers with a "portfolio at a glance" (Campbell, et al., 2004, p. 98). You might want to leave a CD ROM, a DVD, or a web site address containing electronic materials. Some school districts do examine electronic portfolios when reviewing applicants; other school systems may examine them during the interview process (http://webportfolio.info/). Nonetheless, your portfolio is still proof of your achievements and technology competencies in teaching.

As you interview for jobs, remember that employers are looking for qualities and attributes in addition to teaching and learning competencies. Here are some you may want to consider:

- Ability to interact with others
- Ability to solve problems
- Ability to work with others as a team
- Appearance, dress, and grooming
- Communication skills
- Leadership potential
- Mature behavior and judgment
- Personal enthusiasm, poise, flexibility and a sense of humor
- Realistic appraisal of self and self-reflection
- Self-confidence
- Readiness to have several good questions prepared to ask your employer
- Work ethic/ Professional ethical standards

(http://careers.d.umn.edu/cs_handbook/cshandbook_interviewing.html)

Your New Role as Teacher in a Contemporary Society

As you move from student to teacher, we wonder how the development of portfolio, in all its forms, helped you understand the role of a teacher in a complex, challenging, dynamic and world. This was a query on a questionnaire that we asked a number of our interns to see if they felt that developing a portfolio was worth the time and effort it took. The questionnaire (see Figure 11-1) is given regularly to interns at varying intervals in the program, to administrators, and to mentor teachers. Miguel, a junior early childhood major, felt that using the INTASC Principles helped him to consciously think about each principle and what it meant. "Teaching as a profession is not just what a teacher does in the classroom, but [also] includes what a person does outside the classroom." He felt the portfolio process "illustrates the importance of having a well-rounded education." Alexandra noted that each INTASC Principle corresponds to an area where teachers need to be proficient in order to develop successful students.

Students, as a whole, felt that the portfolio process in professional courses was key for the following three reasons: (1) writing lesson plans and reflective narratives; (2) assessment; and (3) reflecting. Learning to write explicit, detailed lesson plans helped them meet the needs of all students. Writing clear reflective narratives forced pre-service students to relate their course assignments and practical field experiences to the principles and standards that all beginning teachers should be able to exhibit.

Assessment was the second area that interns felt was critical. Portfolio development was modeled in education classes as a process that was assessed throughout pre-service teachers' university careers. The continuous attention to portfolio development helped interns understand that learning is a process and that assessment is ongoing. For example, in many lessons, interns were required to assess children before, during, and after instruction. Pre-service teachers saw this connection and understood that "process over product" has significant value in today's classrooms. This recurrent progression helped interns understand that learning to think is a continuous, not a linear activity.

The value of reflection was a third major response from interns. "The reflective narratives are the largest indicators of my understanding of the content in my courses."

How Did the Portfolio Process Demonstrate Your Professional Growth?

Each pre-service teacher felt that the portfolio process helped in a transformation. Every student discussed change. Most students found the process gratifying, not frustrating. "I enjoyed seeing how I grew as a professional." Most students admitted that demonstrating professional growth got easier as they got farther along in the program.

"By the time I got to student teaching semester, I was more familiar with the standards and curriculum."

"My portfolio completely changed from freshman year until now. I've taken out all but one or two of the original artifacts."

"I've learned to take responsibility for my own professional growth because the portfolio is the showcase of all my work. It is important to be able to support what I have included."

"I was amused to see some of the artifacts that I had included from the beginning of my college experience. They showed how much more I know now than I when I began."

"I am able to look at what I have accomplished as an undergrad; learning to be a teacher is [documented] on paper."

"This process has helped me get organized!"

"The process ensures that we, as students, keep the standards in mind when completing assignments."

"Since the INTASC Principles outline the qualities of effective teachers, this process helps me keep that goal in mind."

Connecting Theory to Practice

One goal of portfolio development is to document growth as an emerging teacher. Another is to authenticate and accomplish identified competencies. But looking back to the purposes of portfolio itemized in Chapter 1, we see that the production of a portfolio also offers many levels of personal and professional growth. It places responsibility on the pre-service intern to set goals, foster best practices, engage in collaborative relationships with other professionals, and connect and integrate theory and practice. By doing so, each student is truly able to shape his or her "professional destiny."
Student comments substantiated that this was, indeed, occurring.

"I think some of the artifacts in my portfolio really show how I have learned and am still learning to become a teacher. Developing the portfolio helped me to understand how to apply the INTASC Principles in my teaching."

"I believe the connection to family and community is the basis for a successful teacher and student."

"I felt I was better able to articulate standards and reference data through my experiences and artifacts in the portfolio."

Viewpoints from Administrators

Administrators were asked, "How does the professional portfolio impact the interview process? Do you feel teacher candidates can successfully demonstrate their qualities as an effective teacher through this document?" Comments from administrators corroborated the value of portfolio development.

"Teacher candidates who actively/assertively refer to their portfolios will distinguish themselves as 'data based' learners and leaders because they are referencing data points from their experience. I think the portfolio provides an excellent opportunity for this but only when the candidate takes the initiative to refer to it. Otherwise, it is a giant resume, and the candidate is not perceiving and using it as documented evidence of his/her experiences and knowledge."

"I believe that I received my first administrative promotion (of 3 candidates who were interviewed) as a result of my initiative to share a portfolio of staff development activities I had developed as a teacher leader. It is powerful evidence when initiated by the candidate. Once again, it is the initiative that sends a message that the candidate is building upon prior experiences and using data to support her/his qualifications for the job. That is indicative of a teacher who will seek and use evidence that students are learning."

"I personally prefer, whenever possible, to see you in person, because it's not the work I'm buying—it is you I'm interested in. I want to hear and see you present your work. Your intelligence, enthusiasm, energy, and passion are more important to me than your whole portfolio. Besides, I'm always as little suspicious of the involvement and influence in your work by faculty and fellow students."

"If I'm criticizing your work, it is always meant to be constructive. It also shows me whether you can take criticism. This is an important factor in evaluating your potential to learn. Actually, my criticism is often directed at the faculty who taught you."

"Dress presentably. Speak up and narrate your work. Don't just sit there and wait for questions or comments. Be self-critical. It is one of the most useful traits to be able to evaluate your own work in as objective a way as humanly possible. Tell me what you think is good and what is not so good. I want to know whether you know the difference. Most of all I want to see and hear that you love and live this profession with a passion."

Figure 11-1   Questionnaire

Portfolio Inquires for Interns and Teachers
1. How did the portfolio process help you to understand the role of a teacher in contemporary society? 2. How was your learning in professional courses demonstrated through the portfolio process? 3. How did the insertion of new artifacts each semester demonstrate your proficiency of the INTASC standards? 4. How did the portfolio process help you take on more responsibility for professional growth? 5. What was the strongest standard demonstrated in your portfolio? 6. What standard needed to be more developed in your portfolio? 7. How did the portfolio process demonstrate your professional growth? 8. Did the portfolio have an effective use after your portfolio interview during student teaching? 9. How did the reflective narrative help you connect theory to practice? Did this process help you grow as a teacher? 10. How could your experience through this process be improved? Additional Comments

Portfolio Inquires for Administrators
1. How does the professional portfolio impact the interview process? Do you feel the teacher candidate can successfully demonstrate his or her qualities as an effective teacher through this document? 2. What would you like to add or change about the portfolio? Additional Comments

Activity 11-1

Use the questions above to prepare for an interview. Write thoughtful answers to each question using the INTASC standards as a guide for showing your growth as a professional.

Summary

Each intern in early childhood education needs training in the important process of documenting his or her growth over time. Preparing to become a thoughtful and reflective practitioner is an important aspect of both teaching and learning. Another very important facet of this formative process is getting a job! The portfolio is an important tangible product that provides a visual image of a potential early childhood educator. However, the most important element is your ability to articulate your skills, knowledge, and attitudes to teach in culturally responsive classrooms. In other words, "Can you walk the walk and talk the talk?"

Suggested Web Sites

Two comprehensive sites give authentic examples of interview questions you might encounter.
www.notrain-nogain.com and
http://careers.d.umn.edu/cs_handbook/cshandbook_interviewing.html

These sites prepare job seekers for interviews and careers in education.
www.interviewtutorial.net
http://careers.d.umn.edu/cs_handbook/cshandbook_interviewing.html
www.uwstout.edu/careers/portfolios.shtml
http://www.nationjob.com
http://www.education-world.com/jobs/t_elem_ed.shtml
http://www.academploy.com

References

Campbell, D. M., Cignetti, P. B., Melenyzer, B. J., Nettles, D. H., & Wyman, R. M. (2007). *How to develop a professional portfolio: A manual for teachers* (4th ed.). Boston: Allyn & Bacon.

Developing and using portfolio in interviews. [On-line]
http://careers.d.umn.edu/cs_handbook/cshandbook_interviewing.html
Retrieved on July 28, 2007.

Kimeldorf, M. (1997). *Portfolio power: The new way to showcase all your job skills and experiences*. Princeton, NJ: Peterson's Publishing Group.

Webportfolio.info (2005). [On-line] http://webportfolio.info/ Retrieved November 2, 2006.